Dolce
Memories

❧❦❧

A Rediscovery
of Italian Desserts

Dolce Memories

A Rediscovery
of Italian Desserts

Irene Ritter

FISHER
er
BOOKS™

Publishers: Bill Fisher
                   Howard Fisher
                   Helen V. Fisher

Editor: Helen V. Fisher

Cover design   Josh Young
Cover photograph: © FoodPix

Book design: Edgar H. Allard

Illustrations: David Fischer

Published by Fisher Books
4239 W. Ina Road, Suite #101
Tucson, AZ 85741
(602) 744-6110

Library of Congress
Cataloging-in-Publication Data

Ritter, Irene S.
  Dolce memories : a rediscovery of Italian
Desserts / Irene Ritter
    p.   cm.
  Includes index.
  ISBN 1-55561-070-6: $12.95
  1. Desserts—Italy. 2. Cookery, Italian.
  I. Title.
TTX773.R592   1995
641.8'6'0945—dc20   94-37123
                                 CIP

© 1995 by Fisher Books
Printed in USA
Printing 10 9 8 7 6 5 4 3 2 1

Notice: The information in this book is true and complete to the best of our knowledge. It is offered with no guarantees on the part of the author or Fisher Books. The author and publisher disclaim all liability in connection with use of this book. Fisher Books are available at special quantity discounts for educational use. Special books or book excerpts can also be created to fit specific needs. For details please write or telephone.

Contents

About the Author

Irene Ritter is a Chicago native living in a mountain hamlet in Oregon's Columbia Gorge with her husband, a dog and a cat. Her first cookbook, *The Cobbler Crusade,* expands the notion of fruit cobblers to include savory meat, seafood and vegetable main-dish cobblers.

Dedication

Dedicated with love to my mother,
Carmelina Siracuse Doti.

Acknowledgments

The author wishes to acknowledge the following people: Helen Fisher, for inspiring me to recognize my ethnic heritage; and food editor, Veronica Durie, for her creative assistance and advice.

I would also like to thank Josephine Ciotta Moore, for providing me with Italian translations of recipes; and Cleo Slifer, Jeff Ritter and Jan Sumrain for helping me during the long, but sweet, testing process.

Introduction

When many Americans think of dolci or Italian sweets, they envision espresso bars displaying glass jars of almond biscotti, gelati shops, or a good Italian bakery selling cassata, cannoli or creamy zabaglione. For me, dolci evoke warm and rich memories of my mother's Sunday evening table.

Dolci by Candlelight

On important occasions in my family, dolci or sweets were served around twilight in my mother's dining room, about two hours after Sunday's late-afternoon dinner.

Dolci spreads were put on by Italian-American families who kept a few of Italy's traditions. For our family, it meant times when my mother opted for candlelight, table linen, bone china, silver espresso pots and dolci. It took years for me to discover that these rituals—which I took for granted—were linked to her native Sicily. To Sicilians, dolci call for an exalted degree of table refinement because this is the epitome of a meal.

My mother, Carmelina Siracuse Doti, was 42 when I was born in Chicago in 1954; so she is almost two generations ahead of me. In 1926, she landed on the shores of New York's Ellis Island as a very young child. Her trip began in her hometown of Catania, Sicily.

She grew up as a streetwise child on Chicago's Near West Side, the former Italian-American neighborhood that now houses the University of Illinois at Chicago. Moreover, she learned to blend American tradition with those she had observed from watching her mother, Concetta Conti Siracusa.

My mother's interpretation of dolci evolved into a series of Sunday nights centered around visits from relatives and close friends or family birthdays, Christmas and the steady round of U.S. holidays from Thanksgiving to Labor Day. A stream of Italian-American relatives or friends offered either home-baked creations or some sweet delicacies bought from a Chicago institution, Nuti Bakery on Grand avenue. Established in 1898, the bakery is still owned by members of the Nuti family.

As a table centerpiece, my mother made two miniature pyramids from one dozen of Nuti's cannoli, nobly stacked on a crystal platter. Each horn-shaped pastry shell was stuffed with a filling made from creamy ricotta, candied citron and semisweet chocolate bits. Nuti's trademark, which I loved, was an outside covering of chopped pistachio nuts and coconut.

Behind the rich cannoli, candlelight flickered off my mother's red Venetian liqueur glasses—part of a handful of precious cargo that had landed safely with my grandmother on Ellis Island. Toward the back of the table and stacked near a silver espresso pot were my mother's English bone china cups, saucers and dessert plates—all ready for sumptuous dolci.

Birthdays brought out the best because they mean spiritual holidays for Sicilians. To my mother, they meant a *cassata,* a multi-layered symbolic cake of life or rebirth. On the night before serving the cassata, she would bake its rich pound cake layers in a loaf pan, then fill them with ricotta cream combined with Amaretto. Overnight, the cassata "aged" or "ripened" in a refrigerator, allowing a subtle bath of spirits to sink into the cake. The highlight was watching her frost a cassata at the serving table. Her frostings—usually made with semi-sweet chocolate and espresso—were slightly chilled before being spread in decorative swirls along the entire cake.

In early December, there appeared fig-and-nut cookies or *cucciddati,* another Sicilian classic baked traditionally during the Christmas season. I recall platters with stacks of cucciddati resting on a powdered-sugar floral pattern created with a paper doily. Relatives brought imported tins of Milanese panettone, a dome-shaped, egg-bread filled with candied fruit and nuts. Historians claim their glorious shapes were meant as reflections of Milanese domes.

Around March 19, Nuti Bakery would bake St. Joseph's Cream Puffs or *Bingè Di San Giuseppe* in honor of St. Joseph, a highly favored

Italian saint. Late spring brought out Lenten yeast breads such as the delicately light Neapolitan baba, literally bathed in a savory-sweet rum.

During summer, there would be cool *zabaglione,* a wine cream, topped with fresh fruit and berries. Or a *tiramisu,* literally translated as "pick-me-up," with a Marsala-and-cream-cheese filling (either mascarpone or cream cheese) layered with espresso-soaked sponge cake.

Though surrounded by all these sweet delights, I preferred the tutti-frutti taste of good spumoni in hot July to anything tasting of coffee or wine. My clearest childhood memory of dessert paradise is sitting alone on the front stoop of my porch at night looking up into the stars. There I'm eating a slice of very good spumoni filled with sliced strawberries, chopped pistachio nuts and chocolate bits—all resting daintily on a sheet of pink waxed paper.

Behind the Dolci Rituals

Off to the sideline on our occasional Sunday dolci table lay a humble tin of biscotti, usually ignored.

Memories of that biscotti tin caused me to recall other things I used to take for granted—such as my mother's dolci rituals. Nevertheless, my mother purposely kept her native customs and language a mystery to me. Like many Americans from her generation, she was anxious to become part of the American melting pot. When my mother was a young child, she was deprived of much family history. For her strong anti-Fascist parents, Italy had become a place to forget.

So my search began with sweet memories relayed in broken English by my mother's older sister, Francesca Siracusa Cusumanu, whom I fondly called Zia Frances. She loved reading Dante in Italian and taught me how to bake miniature pizzas by using the insides of jar caps as pizza pans. Zia was old enough to remember better times, the days when her father, Francesco owned a *gelaterie* and bicycle-rental shop on a busy Catanian street corner, and her grandfather, Papa Conti, owned bakeries in cities along Sicily's eastern coast.

At those ice-cream stands and bakeries, one could find Sicily's most treasured food creations—dolci. In fact, the Sicilian's love for sweets dates as far back as the 9th century, when Saracens introduced sugar to the island. Since then, many Sicilians have tied the idea of eating sweets with magical and religious themes. For example, at October's end, street vendors sell candy to celebrate the Fiera dei Morti or Fair of the Dead. And on December 13, or Saint Lucy's Day, my grandfather's native town of Siracusa was traditionally lit with lights and its residents celebrated with bowls of sweet molasses puddings.

Sicilians even attach a certain exalted quality to bread—particularly sweet breads or cakes. For instance, I recall my mother's strange, but graceful, act of gently kissing a slice of stale bread or cake before discarding it—not into the garbage, but to backyard birds. When I asked her the significance of this, she said she had learned it from her mother. But when I asked Zia Frances, I was told that any "proper" Sicilian thinks of bread as holy. In fact, Sicilians once believed they would spend eternity brushing their eyelashes across a floor to pick up every crumb they had wasted on earth.

Years after Zia died, a friend caught me kissing leftover brioche before tossing it to birds flying along the Oregon Coast. In explaining this unusual veneration for bread, I said the act somehow connected me to my Sicilian grandmother who had died many years before I was born, and who passed a few traditions from earlier times down to my mother.

And now, whenever I celebrate a close friend or family member's achievement or birthday, or a holiday, my penchant for supplying dolci connects me to the grandmother I never met, as well as to my mother and aunts—all Italian immigrants.

Like these women, I feel that dolci served by candlelight is the best way to turn an event into a celebration of life.

Dolci in Italy

Italy is far more regionalized than the U.S. or Canada. Thus, many dolci recipe names vary from one town to the next. For example, one version of the Milanese panettone is called *biscieùla*. But in the Valle d'Aosta, *panettone* doesn't mean yeast bread at all; it means almond pastry. A *cassata* in Naples is a type of ice cream, while in Sicily it is a spectacularly rich layer cake much like the one my mother made.

Discovering Dolci in the New World

In attempting to bring 70 dolci recipes from various regions of Italy to the North-American kitchen, I started out with a philosophy held by my mother. She raised four children and worked at a full-time job outsid of the home. She would not spend the time nor money buying ingredients that couldn't be found at a local grocery store.

This doesn't mean traditions need to be compromised. So my approach has been to simplify many of the original Italian recipes, adapting them to include some very good ingredients readily available in North America. Consider my Florentine tart with layers of ricotta and fresh raspberries. Adding raspberries reflects my love for using a fresh and abundant berry found in my Pacific Northwest backyard. This may be breaking tradition in a classic Florentine tart, for the only place fresh raspberries are grown abundantly in Italy is in the Tyrol. But still my basic nut-pastry-and-ricotta filling follows the original idea.

Another example is the addition of pecans to some cookie recipes. This was inspired by my mother's cousin, Pearl Conti, whose family settled in Texas around the mid-1920s. Pearl embraced Southern U.S. cooking. And it didn't take long for her to discover that the Texas state nut—the pecan—goes well with lemon zest in an Italian wreath cookie called a *ciambella*.

Dolci Leggeri

Some of my recipes fall into the category of Dolci Leggeri, lighter desserts with lowered saturated fats.

For instance, in some of the tart or crostata recipes, I combined canola oil with smaller amounts of butter than required in original recipes. The resulting flavorful crusts are every bit as crumbly as those calling for lard, olive oil or butter. In fact, many recipes coming out of Italy today reflect a growing trend toward lowered saturated-fat alternatives. Canola oil, for instance, is gaining steady popularity for cooking and baking.

In many of the Italian cakes, or torte, for example, particularly in the sponge and chiffon-types, I also decreased the number of egg yolks, while increasing egg whites and adding milk and canola oil.

Biscotti
Twice-Baked Cookies

*B*iscotti literally means twice-baked cookies. No other type of Italian cookie is as popular or has as many European counterparts. Among them are British Hardtack, Jewish Mandelbrot and German Zwieback.

As a child, many of my friends living in my ethnically rich Chicago neighborhood had grandmothers or mothers baking the same type of twice-baked cookie, but with different names and shapes. Some were crunchy and flavorful; and some were so hard and dry, for want of a common name, my friends and I named them "chokers."

Now biscotti in glass jars are well-known staples at espresso stands. The biggest draw is the way they hold their shapes when dunked in a beverage. That's because the twice-baked process removes excess moisture, yielding long shelf life and optimum dunking quality.

The dunking beverage of choice for most Italians in Italy is a sweet dessert wine or cappuccino. But I must admit that my American-bred tastes would never settle for anything other than a glass of cold milk.

Shortening and Other Ingredients

Shortening makes a big difference in biscotti texture and taste. To produce a rich flavor, butter is essential, but you don't need a lot of it. A little butter in biscotti goes a long way.

Other ingredients—lemon or orange zest, currants and dried fruits; nuts and seeds; and an array of spices—have been baked into Italian biscotti since the days when sea voyagers like Columbus stored these long-lasting biscuits on ships for months at a time.

Apricot Marsala Biscotti

Biscotti di Albicocca con Marsala

*M*arsala and slivered almonds blend beautifully with the tartness of dried apricot. The almonds and diced apricots yield a very good and chewy texture.

2-1/2 cups all-purpose flour

1-1/2 teaspoons baking powder

1/8 teaspoon salt

1/3 cup butter, room temperature

3/4 cup sugar

2 whole eggs, well beaten

2 tablespoons Marsala

3/4 cup diced dried apricots (almost 1/2 pound)

1/2 cup slivered almonds

Preheat oven to 325F (160C). Coat a medium-size baking sheet with vegetable-oil spray and flour. In a small bowl, mix flour, baking powder and salt with a fork until blended; then set aside dry ingredients.

In a large bowl, with an electric mixer beat butter and sugar together; mix in beaten eggs, Marsala, apricots and almonds until thoroughly blended. Gradually add combined dry ingredients and continue mixing until dough is stiff, but slightly sticky.

To Form and Slice the Biscotti: (See page 14) Using a rubber spatula, turn out dough onto lightly floured working surface. With floured hands, divide dough in half, forming 2 loaves, each measuring about 9 x 2-1/2-inches. Place loaves at least 3 inches apart on baking sheet. Then bake loaves for 30 minutes or until slightly golden brown.

Remove baking sheet from oven, but leave oven at same temperature. Let loaves cool slightly. Using a spatula, carefully transfer loaves from baking sheet to a rack and allow to cool for 5 minutes.

Place loaves on a cutting board. With a serrated knife, cut each loaf diagonally into 1/2-inch slices. Using your thumbs and fingertips, carefully turn each cookie slice over once; then transfer to original baking sheet. Return to oven for 10 minutes.

Remove biscotti from oven and cool slightly; then transfer slices to rack, allowing to cool completely before storing in tightly closed containers.

Makes 22-24 biscotti slices.

Chocolate-Chip Biscotti

Biscotti con Cioccolatini e Cocco

*T*his recipe for a rich-tasting biscotti was inspired by friend's grandmother who baked her *Mandelbrot* with chocolate chips and shredded coconut.

> 2-1/3 cups all-purpose flour
>
> 1-1/2 teaspoons baking powder
>
> 1/8 teaspoon salt
>
> 1/3 cup butter, room temperature
>
> 2/3 cup sugar
>
> 2 whole eggs, well beaten
>
> 2 tablespoons milk
>
> 1-1/2 cups shredded coconut
>
> 1/2 cup semisweet chocolate chips

Preheat oven to 325F (160C). Coat a medium-size baking sheet with vegetable-oil spray and flour.

In a small bowl, mix flour, baking powder and salt with a fork until blended; set aside.

In a large bowl, with an electric mixer beat butter and sugar together; mix in beaten eggs, milk, coconut and chocolate chips until thoroughly blended. Gradually add combined dry ingredients and continue mixing until dough is stiff, but slightly sticky.

To Form and Slice the Biscotti: (See page 14) Using a rubber spatula, turn out dough onto lightly floured working surface. With floured hands, divide dough in half, forming 2 loaves, each measuring about 9 x 2-1/2 inches. Place loaves at least 3 inches apart on baking sheet. Then bake loaves for 30 minutes or until slightly golden brown.

Remove baking sheet from oven, but leave oven at same temperature. Cool loaves slightly. Using a spatula, carefully transfer loaves from baking sheet to rack and allow to cool for 5 minutes. Then place loaves on a cutting board. Using a serrated knife, cut each loaf diagonally into 1/2-inch slices. Using your thumbs and fingertips, carefully turn each cookie slice over once; then transfer to original baking sheet. Return to oven for 10 minutes.

Remove biscotti from oven and cool slightly; then transfer slices to rack, allowing to cool completely before storing in tightly closed containers.

Makes 22-24 biscotti slices.

Lemon-Vanilla Biscotti

Biscotti di Limone e Vaniglia

*V*anilla bean, a plant native to Central America, but revered in many Italian desserts, provides a delicate balance to the lemon zest in biscotti.

2 cups plus 1 tablespoon all-purpose flour

1 teaspoon baking powder

1/2 teaspoon baking soda

1/8 teaspoon salt

2 teaspoons vanilla-bean shavings (3-1/2- to 4-inch bean pod)

1/2 cup butter, room temperature

2/3 cup sugar

2 eggs, well beaten

1 teaspoon lemon zest

1 tablespoon lemon juice

Topping:

Powdered sugar

Preheat oven to 325F (160C). Coat a medium-size baking sheet with vegetable-oil spray and flour. In a medium-size bowl, mix flour, baking powder, baking soda, salt and vanilla shavings with a fork until blended; then set aside dry ingredients.

In a large bowl, with an electric mixer beat butter and sugar together; mix in beaten eggs, lemon zest and lemon juice until thoroughly blended. Gradually add combined dry ingredients and continue mixing until dough is stiff, but slightly sticky.

To Form and Slice the Biscotti: (See page 14) Using a rubber spatula, turn out dough onto lightly floured working surface. With floured hands, divide dough in half, forming 2 loaves, each measuring about 9 x 2-1/2 inches. Place loaves at least 3 inches apart on baking sheet. Then bake for 30 minutes or until slightly golden brown.

Remove baking sheet from oven, but leave oven at same temperature. Cool slightly. Using a spatula, carefully transfer loaves from baking sheet to a rack and allow to cool for 5 minutes. Then place loaves on a cutting board. Using a serrated knife, cut each loaf diagonally into 1/2-inch slices. Using your thumbs and fingertips, carefully turn each cookie slice over once; then transfer to original baking sheet. Return to oven for 10 minutes.

Remove biscotti from oven and cool slightly; then transfer slices to rack, allowing to cool completely. Sprinkle with powdered sugar before storing in tightly closed containers.

Makes 22-24 biscotti slices.

Orange Anise Biscotti

Biscotti di Arance e Anice

Orange and anise seed blend together in this biscotti to create a perfect marriage of flavors. These are meant to be savored during a relaxing late afternoon espresso, coffee or tea.

> 2-1/2 cups all-purpose flour
>
> 1-1/2 teaspoons baking powder
>
> 1/2 teaspoon baking soda
>
> 1/8 teaspoon salt
>
> 2 teaspoons anise seeds
>
> 1/2 cup butter, room temperature
>
> 3/4 cup sugar
>
> 2 whole eggs, well beaten
>
> 2 tablespoons orange zest
>
> 1-1/2 tablespoons orange juice

Preheat oven to 325F (160C). Coat a medium-size baking sheet with vegetable-oil spray and flour. In a small bowl, mix flour, baking powder, baking soda, salt and anise seeds with a fork until blended; then set aside dry ingredients.

In a large bowl, beat butter and sugar together with an electric mixer; mix in beaten eggs, orange zest and orange juice until thoroughly blended. Gradually add combined dry ingredients and continue mixing until dough is stiff, but slightly sticky.

To Form and Slice the Biscotti: (See page 14) Using a rubber spatula, turn out dough onto lightly floured working surface. With floured hands, divide dough in half forming 2 loaves, each measuring 9 x 2-1/2 inches. Place loaves at least 3 inches apart on greased and lightly floured baking sheet. Then bake for 30 minutes or until slightly golden brown.

Remove baking sheet from oven, but leave oven at same temperature. Cool slightly. Using a spatula, carefully transfer loaves from baking sheet to rack and allow to cool for 5 minutes. Then place loaves on a cutting board. Using a serrated knife, cut each loaf diagonally into 1/2-inch slices. Using your thumbs and fingertips, carefully turn each cookie slice over once; then transfer to baking sheet. Return to oven for 10 minutes.

Remove biscotti from oven and cool slightly; then transfer slices to rack, allowing to cool completely before storing in tightly closed containers.

Makes 22-24 biscotti slices.

Hazelnut Biscotti

Biscotti di Nocciole

I prefer hazelnuts to any other kind of nut in this crunchy biscotti for two good reasons. Hazelnuts are native to my Pacific Northwest home and their flavor matches the sweet, but slightly tart, flavor of the added dried currants. This version has a slightly chewier texture than the rest, because I've lowered the amount of shortening and added egg whites.

    2-1/3 cups all-purpose flour

    1-1/2 teaspoons baking powder

    1/8 teaspoon salt

    1/4 cup butter, room temperature

    2/3 cup powdered sugar

    2/3 cup fine hazelnut or walnut crumbs

    2/3 cup dried currants

    2 egg whites, well beaten

Topping:

1-1/2 tablespoons powdered sugar

Preheat oven to 325F (160C). Coat a medium-size baking sheet with vegetable-oil spray and flour. In a small bowl, mix flour, baking powder and salt with a fork until blended; then set aside dry ingredients.

    In a large bowl, with an electric mixer beat butter and powdered sugar together; mix in hazelnuts or walnuts, currants and beaten egg whites. Gradually add combined dry ingredients and continue mixing until dough is stiff.

To Form and Slice the Biscotti: (See page 14) Using a rubber spatula, turn out dough onto lightly floured working surface. With floured hands, divide dough in half, forming 2 loaves, each measuring 9 x 2-1/2 inches. Place loaves at least 3 inches apart on baking sheet. Then bake for 30 minutes, or until slightly golden brown.

Remove baking sheet from oven, but leave oven at same temperature. Cool slightly. Using a spatula, carefully transfer loaves from baking sheet to rack and allow to cool for 5 minutes. Then place loaves on a cutting board. Using a serrated knife, cut each loaf diagonally into 1/2-inch slices. Using your thumbs and fingertips, carefully turn each cookie slice over once; then transfer to original baking sheet. Return to oven for 10 minutes.

Remove biscotti from oven and cool slightly; then transfer slices to rack, allowing to cool completely before sprinkling with powdered sugar and storing in tightly closed containers.

Makes 22-24 biscotti slices.

Toasted Almond Biscotti

Biscotti di Mandorle Arrostite

*T*oasted whole almonds and Amaretto liqueur combine in a chewy, lighter-version biscotti made with egg whites only (no yolks). Top with a combination of powdered sugar and orange or lemon zest for added flavor and color.

> 1 cup whole, raw almonds
>
> 2 cups all-purpose flour
>
> 1-1/2 teaspoons baking powder
>
> 1/8 teaspoon salt
>
> 1/2 teaspoon ground nutmeg
>
> 5 tablespoons butter, room temperature
>
> 2/3 cup plus 1 tablespoon powdered sugar
>
> 2 egg whites, well beaten
>
> 1 tablespoon Amaretto liqueur

Topping:

1-1/2 tablespoons powdered sugar

2 teaspoons orange or lemon zest

To Toast Whole Almonds: Place whole almonds in ungreased heavy skillet and cook over medium heat 5-7 minutes, stirring frequently until nuts turn golden brown. Remove from heat and cool; then chop nuts into coarse crumbs.

Preheat oven to 325F (160C). Coat a medium-size baking sheet with vegetable-oil spray and flour. In a small bowl, mix flour, baking powder, salt and nutmeg with a fork until blended; then set aside dry ingredients.

In a large bowl, with an electric mixer beat butter and powdered sugar together; add almonds, beaten egg whites and Amaretto. Gradually add combined dry ingredients and continue mixing until dough is stiff, but slightly sticky.

To Form and Slice the Biscotti: (See page 14) Using a rubber spatula, turn out dough with floured hands onto lightly floured working surface. Divide dough in half, forming 2 loaves, each measuring 8-1/2 x 2-1/4 inches. Place loaves at least 3 inches apart on baking sheet. Then bake for 30 minutes or until slightly golden brown.

Remove baking sheet from oven, but leave oven at same temperature. Cool slightly. Using a spatula, carefully transfer loaves from baking sheet to rack and allow to cool for 5 minutes. Then place loaves on a cutting board. Using a serrated knife, cut each loaf diagonally into 1/2-inch slices. Using your thumbs and fingertips, carefully turn cookie slice over once; then transfer to baking sheet. Return to oven for 3 minutes.

Remove biscotti from oven and cool slightly. Top first with powdered sugar, then with lemon or orange zest. After biscotti are completely cooled, store in tightly closed containers.

Makes about 22 biscotti slices.

Forming and Slicing Biscotti.

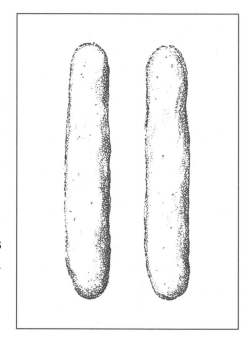

With floured hands divide dough
in half, forming 2 long loaves.

Place loaves at least 3 inches
apart on baking sheet.

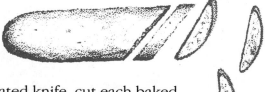

Using a serrated knife, cut each baked
loaf diagonally into 1/2-inch slices and
return to baking sheet.

Traditional Italian Cookies

Pasticcini Tradizionali Italiani

*I*n the 16th century, Catherine de Medici's pastry chefs introduced *Amaretti* or Italian macaroons to the French, who loved them at first bite.

That's not surprising. One sample of these almond-coconut morsels would hook anyone. Yet Amaretti are only one of many enticing cookies so revered in Italy. Italians name them with whimsy, bake them with artistry—and love them for breakfast.

Some cookie titles either reflect their looks or comment on their preparation. One Florentine cookie called Ugly But Good or *Brutti Ma Buoni,* for example, is shaped into a knobby pyramid. Another classic, Nun's Chatter Cookies or *Chiacchiere delle Moniche*, is named for its distinctive chatter—not a crackle—while deep frying.

In Sicily, *taralli* are rings of puffed pastry frosted with sugar. My great grandfather, Franco Conti, a Sicilian baker, frosted his with a sauce made from whisky and anise seed.

As for cookie art, visions of intricate Italian lace can be found in the rich-and-crunchy *Tegole d' Aosta* or tile cookies. But when looking for quintessential flair, look no further than the *Pizzelle,* a delicately thin wafer cookie flavored with anise seed, Amaretto liqueur or cocoa, and embossed into flowery patterns with a special iron.

By contrast, there's the more rustic and substantial Venetian Cornmeal Cookie with pine nuts, called *Gialletti;* and the Sicilian Fig-Nut Bars well-known as *Cucciddati.* Both are so hearty, they help explain why Italians love eating cookies for breakfast.

Italian Macaroons
Amaretti

*A*maretti, also known as *Italian macaroons,* have a distinctively delicate and crunchy outside and a chewy almond-coconut center.

>**5 egg whites**
>**1/2 cup granulated sugar**
>**3/4 lb. coarsely ground almonds**
>**2-1/2 cups shredded coconut**
>**1 teaspoon Amaretto liqueur**

>Topping:
>**3/4 cup granulated sugar**
>**2 teaspoons ground cinnamon**

Preheat oven to 375F (190C). Line a large baking sheet with parchment paper.* In a medium bowl, with an electric mixer whip egg whites while adding 1/2 cup granulated sugar gradually until stiff peaks form. In a large bowl, mix almond crumbs, shredded coconut and Amaretto with a fork. Gently fold meringue into almond-coconut mixture with a rubber spatula until ingredients are thoroughly blended into a soft paste.

Carta al forno is "paper for baking" or parchment paper, a staple item in Italian kitchens.

To Shape Cookies: In a medium bowl, mix granulated sugar and ground cinnamon. Coat your hands with a bit of granulated sugar. Scoop out a tablespoon of meringue-almond paste into one sugar-coated palm and roll into a ball. Then coat ball in bowl of ground cinnamon-sugar. Place 3 inches apart on parchment-lined baking sheets; repeat with remaining batter.

Bake for 12 minutes or until golden brown. Using a wide spatula, transfer Amaretti onto racks to cool completely.

Makes about 32 cookies.

Sicilian Fig-Nut Bars
Cucciddati

*T*hese hearty bars stuffed with dried figs, nuts, raisins and honey are synonymous with winter holidays and tantalizing spicy and sweet baking smells.

Pastry:

1-1/4 cups all-purpose flour

1 teaspoon baking powder

1/4 cup granulated sugar

1/4 cup butter, cut into small pieces

1 whole egg

1 tablespoon orange zest

Filling:

1/2 cup dried mission figs, stems removed

1/2 cup currants

1/4 cup raisins

1/2 cup coarsely chopped walnuts

1 tablespoon brown sugar

1 teaspoon unsweetened cocoa powder

1/4 teaspoon mace

1/8 teaspoon ground cloves

1/8 teaspoon ground cinnamon

2 tablespoons orange zest

1/4 cup honey

Preheat oven to 375F (190C). You will need a large ungreased baking sheet.

To Make Pastry: In a large bowl, combine flour, baking powder and granulated sugar. Using a pastry blender or two knives, cut butter into dry ingredients until mixture becomes slightly crumbly (or use the paddle attachment of a high-powered electric mixer at low speed). Make a well in the center and pour in egg and orange zest. Continue mixing until dough clings together. Add 1 to 2 teaspoons of cold water if needed to hold dough together. Gather dough into a mound. Wrap in foil or plastic wrap and place in refrigerator. Allow to chill for 20 minutes.

To Make Filling: In a food processor, chop dried figs into coarse bits. In a large bowl, using a wooden spoon, mix figs, currants, raisins, walnuts, brown sugar, cocoa powder, mace, cloves, ground cinnamon and orange zest. Pour in honey and continue mixing until well blended.

To Shape Cookies: Remove dough from refrigerator. Divide dough and fig-nut filling into three equal parts. Beginning with one portion, roll on lightly floured surface into a long rectangle, about 1/8 inch thick. Place one third filling lengthwise along center of rectangle. Lift the dough up and over filling to fold in half lengthwise. Seal edges of dough with fingertips and thumbs firmly, tucking ends and seams under. Using a pizza or ravioli cutter or a sharp knife, cut 1-inch slices diagonally.

Transfer each slice, seam-side down, to baking sheet placing at least 2 inches apart. Repeat with two remaining portions of pastry and filling. Bake 13-15 minutes or until golden brown. Cool completely on racks before storing in airtight containers.

Makes about 24 fig-nut bars.

Sardinian Gingerbread Cookies
Abufaus

*I*n Sardinia, abufaus is the Italian version of gingerbread which calls for honey, pine nuts and black pepper. My adaptation of abufaus also features ginger, ground cinnamon and cloves.

- 1 cup butter, room temperature
- 1 cup honey
- 1/2 cup granulated sugar
- 2 whole eggs, well beaten
- 4-3/4 cups all-purpose flour
- 2-1/2 teaspoons baking powder
- 1 cup pine nuts
- 1/8 teaspoon black pepper
- 2-1/2 teaspoons ground ginger
- 1 teaspoon ground cinnamon
- 1/4 teaspoon ground cloves

Topping:
3/4 cup granulated sugar

In a large bowl, with an electric mixer set at high speed mix softened butter, honey and 1/2 cup granulated sugar until mixture is light and fluffy. Lower speed to medium and add beaten eggs until mixture is smooth. Set aside.

In another large bowl, using two forks mix flour, baking powder, pine nuts, pepper, ginger, ground cinnamon and cloves until blended. Using an electric mixer, mix dry ingredients alternately in thirds into butter-honey-egg mixture at medium speed until a soft dough forms. Gather dough into a mound, wrap in foil or plastic wrap and place in refrigerator. Allow to chill for 30 minutes.

To Shape and Bake Cookies: Preheat oven to 350F (180C). You will need a large ungreased baking sheet. Place a bowl of cold water near-by for cleaning your fingers while shaping cookies. Pour 3/4 cup granulated sugar into a medium-size bowl. Coat your hands with a bit of the sugar. Scoop out a tablespoon of chilled dough into one palm of your sugar-coated hands and roll into a ball. Then coat ball in bowl of sugar. Repeat with rest of dough, placing 2 inches apart on baking sheet.

Bake 12-15 minutes or until golden. Transfer to rack to cool completely before storing in airtight containers.

Makes about 48 cookies.

Sardinian Orange-Raisin Cookies
Pasticcini di Arance e Uva Secca

*T*hese wine-raisin cookies with an orange glaze are another Sardinian favorite, often served at weddings. The secret behind the glaze is a pinch of orange flower water.

- 2-1/2 cups all-purpose flour
- 1/4 teaspoon salt
- 1/4 cup granulated sugar
- 1/4 cup brown sugar
- 1 tablespoon orange zest
- 1/2 cup canola oil
- 2 tablespoons butter, cut into small pieces
- 3 tablespoons Marsala
- 3 tablespoons whole or lowfat milk
- 2/3 cup raisins, coarsely chopped

Glaze:
- 1/2 cup powdered sugar
- 1-1/2 tablespoons orange juice
- 1/8 teaspoon orange flower water*

* Orange flower water can be found in Middle Eastern and East Indian food-specialty stores.

In a large bowl, combine flour, salt, brown and granulated sugars and orange zest. Using a pastry blender or 2 knives, cut canola oil and butter into dry ingredients until mixture becomes slightly crumbly (or use the paddle attachment of a high-powered electric mixer set at low speed). Make a well in the center and pour in Marsala, milk and raisins. Continue mixing until dough clings together. Gather dough into a mound, wrap in foil or plastic wrap and place in refrigerator. Allow to chill for 20 minutes.

Preheat oven to 350F (180C). You will need a large ungreased baking sheet.

On a lightly floured surface, roll out dough to about 1/8-inch thick. Using a pizza or ravioli cutter or a sharp knife, cut into 2-inch squares. Arrange on baking sheet, spacing about 1 inch apart. Bake 12-15 minutes or until golden brown. Transfer to rack to cool for about 10 minutes before adding glaze.

To Prepare Glaze: In a small bowl, whisk powdered sugar into orange juice and orange flower water until smooth. Using a pastry brush, brush a thin glaze over slightly warm cookies. Cool completely before storing in airtight containers.

Makes about 66 cookies.

Tiles from Valle d'Aosta

Tegole d'Aosta

*H*ailing from the Valle d'Aosta, tile cookies are perfect for any nut-and-chocolate lover. The name is consistent with their brittle quality and shape.

5 tablespoons butter, cut into small pieces

1/2 cup granulated sugar

1/2 teaspoon vanilla extract

1 tablespoon lemon zest

2/3 cup fine hazelnut crumbs

1/2 cup vanilla cookie crumbs (about 15 cookies)

3 tablespoons all-purpose flour

2 egg whites

Chocolate Glaze:

3 (1 oz.) squares of semisweet chocolate

1/4 cup water

1 cup powdered sugar

Preheat oven to 375F (190C). Line a large baking sheet with parchment paper. In a large bowl, with an electric mixer beat butter, granulated sugar, vanilla and lemon zest together; add hazelnuts, cookie crumbs and flour and continue mixing until ingredients are well blended and crumbly. Be careful not to overbeat or you will create an undesired paste! Set aside.

In a small bowl, whip egg whites with an electric mixer until stiff peaks form. Gently fold meringue into the hazelnut-and-cookie mixture.

To Shape and Bake Cookies: Drop batter, by tablespoonfuls, at least 3 inches apart onto the parchment-lined baking sheets. Using the back of a tablespoon, slightly flatten each cookie. Bake 7-10 minutes. Let cool for about 2 minutes; then gently lift each tile cookie from parchment paper with your fingertips. Transfer tile to rack to cool for an additional 5 minutes before adding glaze.

Instead of using a rack for a flat tile shape, try shaping the warm cookies into curves by placing them over a wine bottle or rolling pin.

To Prepare Glaze: In a double boiler, melt semisweet chocolate into water over medium heat. Whisk powdered sugar into chocolate and water; increase heat to high and whisk until mixture comes to a slight boil. Remove from heat and spoon one teaspoonful of chocolate glaze over each tile. When completely cool, store glazed tiles in airtight containers.

Makes 18-20 tile cookies.

Venetian Cornmeal Cookies

Gialletti or Zaleti

*T*his Venetian classic, a cross between a cookie and a biscuit, features citrus-flavored cornmeal with pine nuts. In Venice, Gialletti are shaped into an odd assortment of shapes such as rings, moons, horseshoes and diamonds.

2/3 cup plus 2 tablespoons butter, cut into pieces

1/3 cup granulated sugar

1 whole egg

1-1/2 tablespoons maple syrup

1 tablespoon orange zest

1-1/2 teaspoons vanilla extract

1-1/2 cups all-purpose flour

1/8 teaspoon salt

1 cup finely ground yellow cornmeal

1/3 cup fine walnut crumbs

1/3 cup pine nuts

In a large bowl, with an electric mixer beat butter, granulated sugar, egg, maple syrup, orange zest and vanilla. Gradually add flour, salt, cornmeal, walnuts and pine nuts until well blended into a dough. Cover with plastic wrap or foil and chill in refrigerator for 20 minutes.

Preheat oven to 375F (190C). You will need a large, ungreased baking sheet.

To Shape Cookies: Remove dough from refrigerator. Divide in half. Beginning with the first half, roll on a lightly floured surface to about 1/8 inch thick. Using a pizza or ravioli cutter or a sharp knife, cut dough into 1-1/2-inch diamond shapes. With a flat spatula, transfer onto baking sheet at least 1 inch apart. Repeat with remaining dough. Bake 12-14 minutes or until golden brown. Transfer to rack to cool completely before storing in airtight containers.

Makes about 30 cookies.

Apricot-Lemon Nut-Bars
Pasticcini di Albicocca e Limone

*M*y recipe is adapted from a classic cookie called *Veneti,* famous in Venice for its lemon icing or apricot jelly. Traditionally, veneti are decorated with a large X of apricot jam, but mine feature a smooth layer of jam with toasted almonds.

> 5 tablespoons butter, cut into small pieces
>
> 2-1/2 tablespoons clover honey
>
> 2 tablespoons powdered sugar
>
> 3 tablespoons lemon juice
>
> 1/2 teaspoon vanilla extract
>
> 1-1/2 cups all-purpose flour
>
> 1 cup fine almond crumbs, divided
>
> 1-1/2 teaspoons butter
>
> 1/2 cup apricot jam
>
> 1 tablespoon lemon zest

In a large bowl, with an electric mixer beat the 5 tablespoons butter, clover honey, powdered sugar, lemon juice and vanilla; gradually add flour and half the almond crumbs (reserving the rest for later). Continue mixing until dough clings together. Gather dough into a mound and wrap in foil or plastic. Place in refrigerator and allow to chill 20 minutes.

Preheat oven to 375F (190C). Line a large baking sheet with parchment paper lightly sprinkled with flour. Remove refrigerated dough. Place directly on the baking sheet, roll out to a 12 x 9-inch rectangle and 1/8 inch thick. Pierce the bottom of the unbaked shell with a fork before baking; then partially bake for 8 minutes.

Meanwhile, melt 1-1/2 teaspoons of butter in a medium skillet over medium heat. With a fork, stir in the remaining half of the almond crumbs. Stir frequently until almond crumbs are slightly golden, about 2 minutes. Then set aside.

Blend apricot jam and lemon zest.

Remove partially baked shell from oven. Immediately spoon apricot jam mixture to cover; then spread toasted almond crumbs evenly over layer of jam. Reduce heat to 350F (180C) and return shell to oven. Bake 7-8 minutes or until golden brown.

Leave shell on parchment paper while transferring onto rack to cool for 5 minutes. Then gently slip parchment paper away from shell and allow to cool for another 5 minutes. Using a wide spatula and your hands, carefully transfer shell to a cutting surface. Using a sharp knife, slice shell into 3-inch bars and return to rack. Allow to cool completely before storing in airtight containers.

Makes 12-14 bars.

Raspberry-Orange Venetian Bars
Pasticcini di Lampone e Arancia

*R*aspberry jam and orange zest combine to make a strong fruit-flavored filling.

- 5 tablespoons butter, cut into small pieces
- 4 tablespoons powdered sugar
- 3 tablespoons orange juice
- 1/2 teaspoon vanilla extract
- 1-1/2 cups all-purpose flour
- 1 cup fine hazelnut crumbs, divided
- 1-1/2 teaspoons butter
- 1/2 cup raspberry jam
- 1 tablespoon orange zest

In a large bowl, with an electric mixer beat 5 tablespoons butter, powdered sugar, orange juice and vanilla; gradually add flour and 1/2 of the hazelnut crumbs (reserving the rest for later) and continue mixing until dough clings together. Gather into a mound and wrap in foil or plastic. Place in refrigerator and allow to chill 20 minutes.

Preheat oven to 375F (190C). Line a large baking sheet with parchment paper lightly sprinkled with flour. Remove dough from refrigerator. Roll dough directly onto the baking sheet to a 12 x 9-inch rectangle and 1/8 inch thick. With a fork, pierce the bottom of the unbaked shel before baking; then partially bake for 8 minutes.

Meanwhile, melt 1-1/2 teaspoons of butter in a medium skillet over medium heat. With a fork, stir in the remaining half of the hazelnut crumbs. Stir frequently until hazelnut crumbs are slightly golden, about 2 minutes. Remove from heat and set aside.

Remove partially baked shell from oven.

Blend raspberry jam and orange zest.

Immediately spoon raspberry jam mixed with orange zest to cover; then spread toasted hazelnut crumbs evenly over layer of jam. Reduce heat to 350F (180C) and return shell to oven. Bake 7-8 minutes or until golden brown.

Leave shell on parchment paper while transferring onto rack to cool for 5 minutes. Then gently slip parchment paper away from shell and allow to cool for another 5 minutes. Using a wide spatula and your hands, carefully transfer shell to a cutting surface. Using a sharp knife, slice shell into 3-inch bars and return to rack. Allow to cool completely before storing in airtight containers.

Makes 12-14 bars.

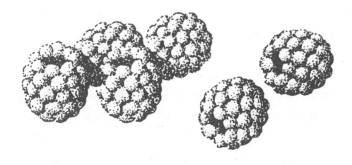

Wreaths

Ciambelle

*C*iambella, a pastry-ring cookie, features a not-so-traditional nut, the pecan, which lends an irresistible flavor.

    1 cup cold butter, cut into small pieces

    1/2 cup powdered sugar

    2 cups all-purpose flour

    1/8 teaspoon salt

    1 cup fine pecan crumbs

    1 teaspoon vanilla

    1 tablespoon lemon zest

Topping:

3 tablespoons powdered sugar

Preheat oven to 375F (190C). You will need a large ungreased baking sheet. In a large bowl, with an electric mixer beat cold butter and 1/2 cup powdered sugar; gradually add flour, salt, pecans, vanilla and lemon zest. Continue mixing until dough is firm enough to handle.

Coat your hands with a bit of granulated sugar. Scoop out 1 tablespoon of cookie dough into the palm of your hands and shape into a rope about 1/2 inch in diameter. Using your fingertips and thumbs, shape the rope into a wreath, crossing ends and tucking seam under. Place seam-side down on baking sheet. Repeat with remaining dough, placing cookies 1-1/2 inches apart.

Bake wreaths 10-12 minutes; then transfer to rack. Wait for about 15 minutes, then sift powdered sugar on top of slightly warm wreaths. Cool completely before storing in airtight containers.

Makes about 32 cookies.

Roll the ball of dough into a rope about 1/2 inch in diameter.

Shape the rope into a wreath, crossing the ends and tucking the seam under.

When baked, sift powdered sugar on top of slightly warm cookies.

Anise Vanilla Pizzelle

Pizzelle di Anice e Vaniglia

*Y*ou will need a pizzelle iron, available at kitchen specialty stores, to make these artistic Italian cookies. My recipe features a lowered-fat version, or dolci leggeri, in two variations: chocolate and Amaretto.

2 cups all-purpose flour

1 cup granulated sugar

1 teaspoon baking soda

1/4 teaspoon salt

1-1/2 teaspoons anise seed

1/2 teaspoon ground nutmeg

2 tablespoons butter, melted and cooled

3 tablespoons plus 1 teaspoon canola oil

1 teaspoon vanilla extract

2 whole eggs

3 egg whites, well beaten

1/4 cup buttermilk

Topping:

1/4 cup powdered sugar

2 tablespoons lemon zest

Heat iron according to manufacturer's instructions. Coat top and bottom cooking surfaces with vegetable-oil spray.

In a large bowl, with two forks lightly mix flour, granulated sugar, baking soda, salt, anise seed and nutmeg. Make a well in the center and pour in cool melted butter, canola oil and vanilla. Using an electric mixer, add whole eggs one at a time, mixing at medium speed. Continue mixing while adding well-beaten egg whites and buttermilk until a smooth and creamy batter forms.

Drop 1 tablespoon of batter onto center(s) of heated pizzelle iron and close. Bake about 45 seconds or until golden brown; carefully loosen pizzelle from iron with fork. Transfer to rack to cool completely. Repeat with remaining batter. After the first cookie is made, the pizzelle iron takes only about 30 seconds to bake remaining pizzelle.

When completely cooled, top with sifted powdered sugar and a sprinkling of lemon zest.

Makes 24 pizzelles.

Variations
Chocolate Pizzelle

Pizzelle al Cioccolato

In topping, replace lemon zest with 1-1/2 tablespoons cocoa powder. Sift onto completely cooled pizzelle.

Amaretto Pizzelle

Pizzelle al Amaretto

Omit vanilla in pizzelle batter, substituting 1 tablespoon Amaretto liqueur.

Nuns' Chatter Cookies
Chiacchiere della Moniche

*T*hese classic pastry cookies, dipped in honey and sprinkled with ground cinnamon and nuts, were so rich they were allegedly forbidden during the 13th century. This recipe is from my Aunt Louisa, who sometimes opted for a colorful topping of honey and tiny multicolored candies called *jimmies* or *sprinkles* when she served "chiacchiere" to children.

> 16 oz. clover honey
>
> 4 tablespoons butter, cut into small pieces
>
> 1-1/2 tablespoons granulated sugar
>
> 1 teaspoon vanilla extract
>
> 4 whole eggs
>
> 2-1/2 cups plus 1-1/2 tablespoons all-purpose flour
>
> 1/4 teaspoon salt
>
> 1/4 teaspoon anise seed
>
> About 1-1/4 cups canola oil for frying
>
> *Variation:* Omit anise seed and substitute 1/4 teaspoon ground nutmeg for a completely different flavor.

Topping Suggestions:

- 1/3 cup fine roasted hazelnut or pecan crumbs
- 1/4 cup granulated sugar mixed with 1/2 teaspoon ground cinnamon
- Jimmies or sprinkles for color

In a medium-size saucepan, heat honey over medium heat to a melting consistency; then simmer on very low heat.

In a large mixing bowl, with an electric mixture beat butter, granulated sugar and vanilla. Add eggs, one at a time until mixture is smooth and frothy. Gradually add flour mixed with salt and anise seed or ground nutmeg and continue mixing until dough is stiff, but slightly sticky.

Using a rubber spatula, turn out dough onto lightly floured working surface. With a lightly floured rolling pin, roll out dough to slightly more than 1/8 inch thick. Using a pizza or ravioli cutter or sharp knife, cut a piece of dough about 4 x 3/4 inches; then carefully twist into a ribbon. Repeat with remaining dough.

In a large, deep skillet, heat oil to 375F (190C). Fry about 7 ribbons at a time until golden brown. Drain on paper towels. Remove honey from heat; then dip each ribbon into warm, melted honey for a quick coating. Place on a serving platter and sprinkle with any of the suggested toppings.

Makes 42-44 twisted bows.

Apricot Kisses

Baci di Albicocca

*W*alnut cookies with a well in the center for a "kiss" of apricot jam and a touch of Marsala.

2/3 cup butter, cut into small pieces

1/2 cup powdered sugar

1/4 cup sweet Marsala

1-1/2 cups all-purpose flour

1 cup fine walnut crumbs

Topping:

1/2 cup granulated sugar

1/4 cup apricot jam

Preheat oven to 350F (180C). You will need a large ungreased baking sheet. In a large mixing bowl, with an electric mixer beat butter, powdered sugar and Marsala until blended. Gradually add flour and walnuts; continue mixing until dough is firm.

To Shape Cookies: Pour 1/2 cup granulated sugar into a small bowl. Coat your hands with a bit of granulated sugar. Scoop out a tablespoon of cookie dough into the palm of your sugar-coated hands and shape into a ball; then roll into the bowl of sugar. Place 1-1/2 inches apart on baking sheet. Using your fingertips, make a well in the center of each cookie; fill with apricot jam.

Bake 15 minutes; then transfer to rack. Cool completely before storing in airtight containers.

Makes about 24 cookies.

Ugly but Good
Brutti ma Buoni

From Tuscany comes Ugly but Good, the literal descriptions of these cookies in Italian. These knobby, pyramid-shaped drop cookies are chewy and crunchy at once because of the dried pineapple and chopped walnut.

1/2 lb. (8 oz.) almond paste

1 egg white

1/2 cup finely chopped dried pineapple

1/3 cup coarsely chopped walnuts

Preheat oven to 300F (150C). Line a large baking sheet with parchment paper or coat with vegetable-oil spray. In a food processer using a steel blade, mix almond paste and egg white until blended; add pineapple and walnuts and continue mixing until just blended.

To Shape Cookies: Drop the dough by 1/2 tablespoonfuls 1 inch apart on prepared baking sheet. Using fingertips and thumbs, pinch into pyramid shapes. Bake for 25 minutes or until golden brown. Cool on baking sheet (not rack) completely before storing in airtight containers.

Makes about 24 cookies.

Conti's Taralli
Taralli di Conti

*T*aralli are meant to be served soon after preparation

> 1/2 (17-1/4 oz.) package frozen puff pastry, thawed (1 sheet)
> 1 tablespoon whiskey
> 2 teaspoons anise seed
> Icing:
> 2-1/2 tablespoons butter
> 2 teaspoons whiskey
> 1 cup powdered sugar
> 2 tablespoons hot water

Preheat oven to 350F (180C). You will need a large ungreased baking sheet. Unfold pastry and cut into strips 5 x 1/2 inches. No rolling of puff pastry is necessary for this recipe. Shape strips into rings, crossing ends and tucking seams under; then place about 1-1/2 inches apart on baking sheet. Using a pastry brush, brush carefully with whiskey; then sprinkle a tiny portion of anise seed on each cookie.

Bake 15 minutes or until golden brown. While cookies are baking, in a medium saucepan over medium heat melt butter in 2 teaspoons whisky. Whisk in powdered sugar and 1 tablespoon of water at a time. Continue whisking until mixture is smooth and syrupy. Keep over very low heat until cookies are finished baking.

Using a spatula, remove cookies and transfer to rack. Immediately brush warm icing on each cookie and serve.

Makes about 30 cookies.

Candy and Fresh Fruit

Confetti e Frutta Fresca

Sometimes in winter, after a long Sunday evening meal, my father would crack walnuts, hazelnuts, almonds and pecans into a wooden bowl. The bowl also contained dried figs imported from Greece and cold Mandarin oranges.

Next to the wooden bowl was an Italian ceramic bowl, piled high with blood-red oranges from Sicily and prickly pears from Arizona. But the precious produce was upstaged by a round confection called *Panforte di Siena,* studded with whole-roasted almonds, candied orange and citron, and baked with a cache of aromatic spices. Waiting for slices seemed to take eternity. And do did my father's nut-cracking ritual.

My parent's kitchen scene encapsulated the Italian love for family sharing and quality time, and how they tied them to a love for sweets. It's a love dating back to the seventh century when the Arabs had already made their mark on Sicilian cuisine. Along with teaching Sicilians how to candy fruit, the Arabs left a rich legacy of confections, starting with the notable *Cubbaita,* or honey-sesame-seed brittle.

This classic confection is typically served alongside fresh fruit. And fruit entrees may range from the refreshingly cold Sicilian Oranges, bathed in caramelized, spiced orange peels, to the warm and sublime Stuffed Peaches or *Pesche Ripiene.* They may be served for brunch or as a middle course for refreshing the palate.

Sesame Brittle with Almonds
Cubbaita di Mandorle

An old Sicilian custom: Before baking this brittle, use reserved half of squeezed lemon as a spatula to smooth mixture along cookie sheet. The idea is to squeeze any residual juice out of the lemon onto the brittle or cubbaita.

Almond-Honey-Sesame Mixture

1-1/2 cups slivered almonds

2/3 cup honey

2/3 cup brown sugar

1/4 cup light corn syrup

1 cup sesame seeds

1-1/2 tablespoons butter

**Juice from one lemon (3 tablespoons)
    (reserve half of squeezed lemon.)**

1 tablespoon lemon zest

1 teaspoon baking soda

Preheat oven to 250F (120C). Spray vegetable oil over a large baking sheet (17-1/4 x 11-1/2 x 1 inch.) Place slivered almonds in ungreased skillet and cook over medium heat 3-5 minutes, stirring frequently until nuts turn golden brown. Remove from heat and cool.

In a large saucepan, combine honey, brown sugar, corn syrup, sesame seeds, toasted almonds, butter, lemon juice and lemon zest. Cook over medium heat, stirring occasionally until mixture reaches 240F (120C) on candy thermometer. Then stir constantly until mixture reaches 325F (160C), or until a tiny amount of mixture dropped into cold water becomes hard and brittle. Immediately remove from heat; quickly stir in baking soda.

Pour almond-honey-sesame mixture onto baking sheet. Using the reserved half of squeezed lemon as a spatula, spread mixture evenly along baking sheet. Squeeze excess juice onto surface while smoothing. When partially cooled, but still pliable, cut brittle into 1-1/2-inch-wide strips, then cut again diagonally to form diamond-shaped pieces.

Store the cubbaita between layers of wax paper in large covered plastic container or cookie tin.

Makes about 60 diamond-shaped pieces of brittle.

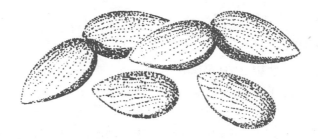

Christmas Fruitcake Candy
Panforte di Siena

Christmas in the Siena province of Tuscany means displays of *pan-forte,* translated in Italian as strong bread. But Panforte di Siena is so chock full of fruit and nuts, it seems to fall into the category of a fruit-and-candy confection. This recipe's origins date back to a Medieval spiced-and-sweetened bread made with dried fruit. Panforte have a long shelf life and are perfect as holiday gifts.

    1 cup coarsely chopped walnuts

    1 cup whole unblanched almonds

    3/4 cup diced candied orange peel

    3/4 cup diced candied citron

    1 teaspoon ground cinnamon

    1/2 teaspoon anise seed

    1/4 teaspoon ground cloves

    1/4 teaspoon nutmeg

    1/2 cup all-purpose flour

    1/2 cup clover honey

    1/2 cup packed brown sugar

    3 tablespoons butter

Preheat oven to 300F (150C). Liberally coat a 9-inch springform cake pan (with removable bottom) with vegetable-oil spray. Line bottom with parchment paper, then lightly coat paper with vegetable-oil spray and flour as a surface for the confection.

In a large bowl, mix walnuts, almonds, orange peel, citron, cinnamon, anise seed, cloves, nutmeg and flour until well blended. Set aside.

In a large saucepan over high heat, combine honey, brown sugar and butter, stirring constantly until mixture comes to a boil. Immediately reduce heat to low and simmer for 1 minute. Pour hot honey-and-brown-sugar mixture into dried fruit and nuts; stir ingredients thoroughly with a wooden spoon. Pour into prepared cake pan and spread evenly with a rubber spatula.

Bake in preheated oven for 30 minutes, then cool thoroughly. When cooled, carefully lift confection and parchment paper from the cake pan's removable bottom to release from bottom and sides. Then, lifting cake by its parchment paper with your thumbs and fingertips, invert cake onto a serving platter. Using a sharp knife, slice into pencil-thin portions. Store in an airtight container or wrap tightly.

Makes one 9-inch-round confection.

Candied Citrus Peel

Frutta Candita

*W*ith only one large saucepan, you can create candied citrus peel, a delicious candy and a filling for panettone and biscotti.

> **Peel 5 medium-size oranges or 4 large grapefruit
>   or a combination 4 cups of citrus**
>
> **12 cups cold water, divided**
>
> Sugar-Honey Glaze:
>
> **2 cups granulated sugar, divided**
>
> **1/2 cup honey**
>
> **1-3/4 cup water**

Score the citrus in quarters and remove peels. Cut into 3/8-inch-wide strips. In a large saucepan, bring 6 cups of the cold water and peel to boil (reserving the other half of the water for later); boil uncovered for about 10 minutes. Drain peels in a colander and rinse with cold water.

Using the same saucepan, repeat process of boiling peel with remaining 6 cups of water. Once again allow the peels to boil uncovered for 10 minutes; then drain and rinse.

Using the same saucepan, start the sugar-honey glaze by bringing 1 cup of sugar (reserving the rest for later), honey and water to a boil, stirring frequently. Boil for one minute; then add drained peel and reduce heat to low, allowing orange peels to simmer in sugar-honey glaze for 40 minutes, stirring frequently. Drain excess glaze from peels in a colander. Then transfer peels to a large bowl and toss with the remaining 1 cup of sugar.

Spread peels on waxed paper in a single layer to cool. Then store in covered containers in refrigerator until ready to eat or add to recipes for panettone or biscotti.

Makes about 4 cups candied citrus peel.

Basic Italian Meringue
with Pistachios and Cinnamon
Meringa Italiana con Pistacchio e Cannella

*T*his frosting or dip made with pistachios and cinnamon is the perfect partner to fresh strawberries, raspberries, plums, peaches or bananas.

> **1/2 cup brown sugar**
>
> **1/4 cup corn syrup**
>
> **2 tablespoons water**
>
> **2 egg whites**
>
> **1 teaspoon vanilla extract**
>
> **2 tablespoons coarsely chopped pistachios**
>
> **1/2 teaspoon cinnamon**

Blend brown sugar, corn syrup and water in a medium-size saucepan. Cover and bring to a boil over medium heat; then reduce heat to medium low and continue simmering 5-7 minutes, without stirring, to 242F (about 117C) on candy thermometer. Mixture will be syrupy.

While mixture is simmering, with an electric mixer beat egg whites in a large mixing bowl until stiff peaks form. Slowly pour corn syrup and brown-sugar mixture into meringue while beating continuously on medium speed. Add vanilla. Increase speed to high and continue beating for 10 minutes or until stiff and very glossy peaks form.

Using a rubber spatula, fold pistachios into meringue. Spoon onto a serving bowl and sprinkle top with cinnamon. Makes almost 3/4 cup meringue.

Stuffed Peaches
Pesche Ripiene

A Piedmont classic in Italy and often served on the tables of Italian Americans is simple to prepare. Here fresh, ripe peaches are stuffed with coconut cookies or macaroons, topped with Amaretto liqueur then baked for a short time in the oven.

6 medium ripe peaches

6 tablespoons apricot preserves

**6 tablespoons coarsely crushed coconut cookies
   or macaroons**

6 tablespoons Amaretto liqueur

Heavy or whipping cream

Preheat oven to 350F (180C). Coat a 13 x 9-inch baking pan with vegetable-oil spray.

Halve peaches and remove pits, but leave peel. Arrange peaches in baking pan. Into each peach cavity spoon 1/2 tablespoon apricot preserves and 1/2 tablespoon crushed coconut cookies or macaroons. Top with a drizzle of 1/2 tablespoon Amaretto. Lightly fleck each peach half with vegetable-oil spray.

Bake for 15 minutes. Remove pan from oven. Cool 12-15 minutes. Serve warm with a bowl of cream to pour over individual servings.

Makes 12 servings.

Sicilian Oranges
Arance alla Siciliana

❦

A most refreshing dessert, a brunch item or a middle course for refreshing the palate are three occasions for serving Sicilian Oranges. Here, large oranges are doused with a zesty caramelized orange-peel bath, then topped with toasted coconut.

2/3 cup shredded coconut

6 large navel oranges

1-3/4 cups granulated sugar

Pinch of ground cloves

To Toast Coconut: Sprinkle shredded coconut in an ungreased heavy skillet over medium-low heat. Stir constantly until golden brown—about 5 minutes. Remove from heat and set aside.

To Prepare Oranges: Using a small serrated knife or an orange peeler, peel oranges, removing only the colored peel. Discard white pith. Set oranges (loosely covered) in refrigerator.

Cut peel into thin strips or shred julienne style in a food processor. In a medium-size saucepan, completely immerse peel in cold water. Bring to a boil; remove from heat and drain, reserving 1/3 cup liquid.

In a large heavy skillet, combine sugar, reserved orange-peel water and ground cloves. Stir over medium heat until sugar dissolves; then reduce heat to low and simmer until mixture begins to caramelize— 20-30 minutes over low heat, stirring occasionally. When sugar mixture is the color of maple syrup, remove from heat. Add cooked shredded peel and stir until peel is completely coated with syrup. Remove from heat and set aside to cool until slightly lukewarm.

Remove oranges from refrigerator. Use a sharp knife to cut any pith or white membrane from outside of each orange. Cut each orange into quarters. Then arrange oranges on a large serving platter. Pour lukewarm syrup-and-peel mixture over oranges. Sprinkle toasted coconut on top and cover loosely. Refrigerate 2 hours before serving.

Makes 6 servings.

Stuffed Pears

Pere Ripiene

───※───

*F*rom the Piedmont region come the Martin secco pears, frequently used in Stuffed Pears or *Pere Ripiene.* Here pears are stuffed with creamy Gorgonzola cheese and walnuts, then chilled. Besides adding a piquant flavor, the lemon helps keep the pears from turning brown.

6 medium, ripe pears

2-1/2 tablespoons lemon juice.

1 cup (1 lb.) Gorgonzola cheese

**2 tablespoons plus 1 teaspoon half-and-half
    or whole milk**

Walnut-Cinnamon Mixture

1/2 cup walnut crumbs

1 teaspoon ground cinnamon

Leaving stems and peel on pears, cut them in half; remove seeds and about 1 tablespoon of pear pulp to create a cavity. Using a pastry brush, coat the insides of each half with lemon juice.

In a large bowl, beat the Gorgonzola and half-and-half or milk just until smooth enough to spread. Using a rubber spatula, spoon cheese mixture into each pear cavity.

Combine walnuts and cinnamon. Sprinkle each pear half with about 2 teaspoons finely chopped walnut-and-cinnamon mixture. Chill for at least 1-1/2 hours or until ready to serve.

Makes 12 servings.

Sweet Bread
Pan Dolce

*A*t first the idea of stuffing an Italian sweet bread with ingredients such as dried pineapple or cranberries seemed too far away from tradition. But then I remembered a story told to me by my father's sister, Louisa Doti Angelico. It happened when my father was eight years old and living in Basilicata, a Southern-Italian region near the Gulf of Taranto. He saw a bag of orange peels discarded near a public inn. Oranges, plentiful in many other areas in Italy, were scarce in Basilicata, a poor, mountainous region with little plain land available for crops. So my father's bag of peels was offered as precious booty to my grandmother, Irena Salvignola Doti, who gratefully kneaded the orange peels into her *panettone*.

In true Southern-Italian form, Irena's sweet egg breads were shaped into very humble, but rich-tasting loaves. They were a far cry from the famous, dome-shape Milanese panettone that industrialist Angelo Motto began baking in 1921.

So, I thought if my grandmother made do with what was available, why couldn't I adopt a similar approach and use readily available dried fruits? Or fashion panettone into different shapes? After all, before Motto's domes, panettone were shaped into loaves much like my grandmother's.

That led to experimenting with different baking pans. First, I compared dome-shape panettone baked in a deep Charlotte Mold to panettone baked in a Bundt pan or a large ring mold. I found that either a Bundt pan or ring mold allows for a more even distribution of heat, yielding a richer taste and texture and a lofty enough dome for my tastes. I also discovered that my grandmother's loaves work best for sealing in syrupy fillings, such as a fruit-nut-and-rum filling in the Pineapple-Walnut Panettone, or *Panettone con Ananas e Noci*.

Finally, I discovered that some classic recipes are best left untouched, such as *Babà*, a Neopolitan feathery-light yeast cake bathed in savory dark rum and sweet spices.

Apricot-Almond Panettone
Panettone Ripieno con Albicocca e Mandorle

*A*lmost a cross between a sweet bread and a confection, this dense loaf emits a perfume of apricots and almond while baking.

Apricot Purée Filling:
3/4 cup chopped dried apricots

1/2 teaspoon lemon juice

1/4 cup granulated sugar

1/4 teaspoon almond extract

1/4 cup reserved liquid for puree

Panettone:
1 package (1/4 oz.) active dry yeast

1/4 cup warm water (105F)

2-1/2 to 3-1/2 cups all-purpose flour

1 cup granulated sugar

1/4 teaspoon salt

3 egg yolks, well beaten

1/2 cup vanilla yogurt

1/2 cup melted butter, room temperature

1/2 teaspoon almond extract

Almond Filling:
4 oz. almond paste, rolled to 12 x 1-1/2 inches

Topping:
1 to 2 tablespoons powdered sugar

Place apricots in a small bowl; cover with warm water. When softened, drain, reserving 1/4 cup liquid. In a food processor, purée chopped apricots, lemon juice, 1/4 cup granulated sugar, almond extract and reserved liquid from the apricots. Chill in refrigerator until ready to assemble panettone.

To Prepare Panettone: In a cup, dissolve yeast in warm water and set aside. In a large bowl, combine flour, granulated sugar and salt. Add beaten egg yolks; then blend in yogurt, melted butter and almond extract. Stir in dissolved yeast and continue mixing with a wooden spoon until ingredients are well blended, then continue mixing with your hands to create a smooth and soft dough.

Turn dough out on a lightly floured surface and knead until smooth and satiny, about 5 minutes. Place in a warm bowl coated with vegetable-oil spray; immediately turn dough so that top is lightly coated with oil.

Cover and let rise in a warm place for about 2 hours or until dough is puffy or rises 2-1/2 to 3 inches. Dough will not double in bulk.

To Shape and Assemble Panettone: Lightly coat a 3-quart ring mold, Bundt pan or ringed springform pan with vegetable-oil spray.

On a lightly floured surface, punch down dough and knead 8-10 times. With a rolling pin, roll dough into a large circle about 18 inches in diameter. Fit the circle of dough into the bottom and sides of ring mold, allowing it to hang over the outside.

Cut the long strip of almond paste into shorter pieces to fit inside and around bottom of dough-lined pan.

Remove chilled apricot filling. Spread apricot on top of almond paste filling to cover, not touching sides of dough, or it will not seal.

Lift the hanging outside edges of dough, lap and fold over filling; seal and press with fingertips to inside ring of dough. Cut an X in dough covering center of the ring and fold each triangle back and over ring. Don't worry if a small amount of apricot filling leaks through.

Cover and let sit in a warm place until dough rises halfway to the top of pan, about 30 minutes.

Preheat oven to 350F (180C). Place panettone on middle rack of oven for 30 to 40 minutes or until top is golden brown and a wooden pick inserted comes out clean. If it browns too quickly, loosely cover top with foil. Cool for 10 minutes, remove from pan and place on a rack to cool completely. Sprinkle with powdered sugar before serving.

Makes 10-12 servings.

Cranberry-Almond Panettone

Panettone con Mirtilli e Mandorle

*M*y panettone is Bundt-shaped with cranberries, slivered almonds and currants. The topping is my Aunt Louisa's very simple recipe for a vanilla-currant glaze.

1 (1/4 oz.) package active dry yeast

1/4 cup warm water 105F (40C)

3/4 cup warm milk 105F (40C)

3/4 cup butter

1/2 cup plus 2 tablespoons granulated sugar

4 eggs, room temperature

4 cups all-purpose flour

1 teaspoon salt

1 cup dried, sweetened cranberries

1/2 cup dried currants

1/2 cup slivered almonds

Currant Glaze:

1/3 cup butter

2 cups powdered sugar

1-1/2 teaspoons vanilla extract

2-3 tablespoons dried currants

3-4 tablespoons hot water

In a small bowl dissolve yeast in warm water; add warm milk and stir gently until blended. Set aside. In a large bowl, with an electric mixer cream 3/4 cup butter and granulated sugar until smooth. Add whole eggs one at a time, then yeast-milk mixture. Mix until ingredients are well blended. Gradually add flour and salt and continue beating at low speed until batter is slightly sticky. Using a wooden spoon, gently stir cranberries, 1 cup currants and slivered almonds into sticky batter.

Lightly coat a Bundt pan with vegetable-oil spray. Spoon batter into pan and spread evenly. Cover and let batter rise in a warm place until doubled in bulk, about 2 hours. Using a wooden spoon, gently stir down risen batter. Loosely cover and let rise again until batter reaches about 1/4 inch from the top of Bundt pan.

Preheat oven to 375F (190C). Bake batter 45-50 minutes or until a wooden pick inserted comes out clean. Let cool in pan for about 20 minutes; then gently loosen cake by running knife along tube and sides of Bundt pan. Immediately invert cake out of Bundt pan onto rack to cool for another 15 minutes before topping with glaze.

To Prepare Vanilla-Currant Glaze: In a medium-size saucepan, melt 1/3 cup butter over medium heat. Whisk in powdered sugar, vanilla and 2-3 tablespoons currants; then increase heat to medium-high and stir in water, 1 tablespoon at a time, until glaze is smooth and syrupy.

Makes 10-12 servings.

Lemon-Ricotta Filled Panettone
Panettone Ripieno con Ricotta e Limone

A rich, moist bread with a center of ricotta and cream cheese, finished with a strawberry-jam topping.

Panettone:

1 (1/4 oz.) package active dry yeast

1/4 cup warm water 105F (40C)

2-1/2 to 3-1/2 cups all-purpose flour

3/4 cup granulated sugar

1/4 teaspoon salt

3 egg yolks, well beaten

1/2 cup vanilla yogurt

1/2 cup melted butter, room temperature

Lemon-ricotta Filling:

1/2 cup cream cheese, softened

4 oz. ricotta cheese

1 whole egg

3 tablespoons powdered sugar

1 tablespoon lemon zest

1/2 teaspoon vanilla extract

Topping:

1/2 cup strawberry jam

In a small bowl, dissolve yeast in warm water and set aside. In a large bowl, combine flour, granulated sugar and salt. Add beaten egg yolks; then blend in yogurt and butter. Stir in dissolved yeast and continue mixing with a wooden spoon until ingredients are well blended, then continue mixing with your hands to create a smooth and soft dough.

Turn dough out onto a lightly floured surface and knead until smooth and satiny, about 5 minutes. Place in a warm bowl coated with vegetable-oil spray; immediately turn mound of dough so top is lightly coated with oil. Cover and let rise in a warm place for about 2 hours or until dough is puffy or rises 2-1/2 to 3 inches. Dough will not double in bulk.

To Assemble Panettone: Lightly coat a 3-quart ring mold, Bundt pan or ringed springform pan with vegetable-oil spray.

On a lightly floured surface, punch down dough again and knead 8-10 times. With a rolling pin, roll dough into a large circle about 18 inches in diameter. Fit the circle of dough along the bottom and sides of the ring mold, allowing it to hang over the outside. Set aside.

In a large bowl, with an electric mixer beat cream cheese, ricotta cheese, egg, powdered sugar, lemon zest and vanilla until smooth and creamy. Pour cheese filling into ring mold.

Lift the hanging outside edges of dough, lap and fold over filling; then seal and press with fingertips to inside ring of dough. Cut an X in dough covering center of the ring mold and fold each triangle back and over ring. Don't worry if a small amount of cheese filling leaks through.

Cover and let sit in a warm place until dough rises halfway to the top of pan, about 30 minutes.

Preheat oven to 350F (180C). Place panettone on middle rack of oven for 30 to 40 minutes or until top is golden brown and a wooden pick inserted into panettone comes out clean. If it becomes brown too quickly, cover top of ring loaf loosely with foil. Allow to cool for 10 minutes, remove from pan and place on a rack to cool completely.

When bread has completely cooled, heat strawberry jam in a small saucepan until melted. Remove from heat and spread warm jam over top and sides of panettone with a pastry brush.

Makes 10-12 servings.

Neopolitan Rum Cake
Babà

A light yeast cake soaked in a savory-sweet rum sauce with cloves, cinnamon stick, vanilla and rum.

Yeast Cake:

1/4 cup milk

1/4 cup butter

1 (1/4 oz.) package active dry yeast

1 teaspoon granulated sugar

2 egg yolks

1/4 cup granulated sugar

1 whole egg

1/2 teaspoon lemon zest

2 tablespoons black or golden raisins

1-3/4 cups all-purpose flour, sifted

Rum Sauce:

1 cup water

1 cup sugar

2 slices lemon

1 slice orange

2-inch length of cinnamon stick

1/2 teaspoon vanilla extract

1 whole clove

1/4 cup dark rum

Coat a Bundt pan with vegetable-oil spray and set aside. In a large saucepan, heat milk and butter until melted. Set aside from heat to cool. When milk temperature cools down to 105-115F (40-45C), sprinkle yeast and sugar into milk mixture. Let stand 3 to 5 minutes. Using an electric mixer, beat in egg yolks while gradually adding granulated sugar. Then add whole egg, lemon zest, raisins and sifted flour and continue mixing until well blended.

Spoon into prepared Bundt pan; cover and let rise in a warm place until doubled in bulk, about 1 hour. Then gently stir the risen batter down with a wooden spoon. Cover and let rise again for 30 minutes or until doubled in bulk.

Preheat oven to 350F (180C). Bake for 20 minutes or until a wooden pick inserted comes out clean. Set aside to cool for 5 minutes, then invert cake out of Bundt pan onto rack to cool completely. When completely cool, pour cooled rum sauce over cake. Let set 1 hour before serving.

Tip: Use waxed paper beneath cake to catch rum sauce drippings.

To Prepare Rum Sauce: In a saucepan bring water, sugar, lemon and orange slices, cinnamon stick, vanilla and clove to a boil, stirring constantly. Reduce heat to low and simmer 6-7 minutes. Strain lemon and orange slices, cinnamon stick and clove from sauce; then stir in dark rum. Set rum sauce aside to cool until you're ready to soak cake.

If you want to prepare the cake in advance, just wrap in foil and freeze. Thaw completely before soaking in rum sauce.

Makes 10-12 servings.

Pineapple-Walnut Panettone

Panettone con Ananas e Noci

A timeless version of a panettone is stuffed—like a calzone. But a fresh idea for a filling combines dried pineapple, walnuts and rum. Because more time and preparation are required in this recipe, I make at least two loaves, particularly during winter holidays, so I can share them as gifts.

1 cup golden raisins

1/4 cup dark rum

1/4 oz. or 1 package of active dry yeast

1/4 cup warm water 105F (40C)

1/8 teaspoon granulated sugar

1/2 teaspoon salt

3/4 cup packed brown sugar

1/8 teaspoon nutmeg

1 tablespoon lemon zest

1 cup milk, lukewarm 105F (40C)

4 whole eggs, slightly beaten

6-1/2 to 7 cups all-purpose flour

1/2 cup melted butter, room temperature

Filling:

8 slices dried pineapple

1-1/3 cups powdered sugar

1/4 cup whole milk or lowfat milk

1/4 cup butter, melted

1/2 cup dark rum

1 cup coarsely chopped walnuts

1 cup golden raisins

In a small bowl combine raisins and rum; set aside. In a large bowl, dissolve yeast in warm water and allow to stand 5 minutes or until surface is frothy. Stir in granulated sugar, salt, brown sugar, rum-soaked raisins, nutmeg, lemon zest, lukewarm milk and eggs. Beat with an electric mixer until milk mixture is well blended. Change to dough hook and add flour gradually to milk mixture, beating at low speed. Increase speed to medium; add 1/2 cup cooled melted butter. Continue mixing until a stiff dough forms.

Give the dough a final kneading by hand. On a lightly floured surface, knead dough until smooth and satiny. Place in a warm bowl coated with vegetable-oil spray; then immediately turn mound of dough so that the top is lightly coated with oil. Cover and let rise in a warm place for about 2 hours or until almost doubled in bulk. Test by inserting two fingers about 1/2 inch into risen dough. If indentations remain, the dough is ready to shape. Punch down dough several times and return to warm bowl; cover and let rise for 1/2 hour.

Place pineapple in a small bowl, cover with warm water. When softened, drain well and dice. When dough has almost completed its second rising, begin pineapple-walnut filling. In a medium saucepan, whisk powdered sugar into milk, 1/4 cup melted butter and dark rum over low to medium heat until smooth and syrupy, 3 to 4 minutes. Stir in pineapple bits, walnuts and golden raisins. Continue stirring for

(Recipe continued on page 64)

about 1 minute until smooth and syrupy. Then set aside to cool until ready to assemble panettone.

To Assemble Panettone Loaves: Preheat oven to 350F (180C). Lightly coat a large baking sheet with vegetable-oil spray.

On a lightly floured surface, divide dough into two equal portions. Roll each portion out to about a 10 x 8-inch rectangle.

Beginning with first rectangle, spoon one third of the cooled pineapple-walnut filling lengthwise along center of rectangle, leaving a 1-inch margin for sealing edges.

Lift dough up and over filling to fold in half lengthwise. With finger-tips seal dough edges firmly, tucking ends and seams under. Repeat with remaining dough and another one third of filling; then transfer both loaves onto baking sheet, seam-side down, 4 inches apart. Set the remaining one third filling aside to use as topping.

Bake loaves on middle oven rack 25-30 minutes or until wooden pick inserted in middle comes out clean. If browning too quickly, cover loaves loosely with foil. Remove from oven; transfer onto rack to cool. When loaves are completely cooled, heat the remaining one third of pineapple-walnut filling in saucepan until syrupy. Spoon over both loaves. Cut into 1/2-inch-wide slices and serve.

Makes 2 rectangular loaves.

Optional:
Before slicing, top each loaf with maraschino cherries for holiday color.

Classic Cakes
Torte

*O*n my mother's table the crowning glory amid an assortment of tempting desserts was a multi-layered cake called *Sicilian cassata,* perhaps one of the oldest of classic Italian cakes.

Carrying the theme of rebirth, a true cassata must go through a ripening process to allow the fillings to soak through the cake's layers. Early variations were baked in Arabian bowls called *qas'ah* and used by nuns in Sicilian convents. Each nun would take her turn as mistress of the pastry oven, applying her brand of artistry onto a layer cake made with flower petals fashioned out of striped-green marzipan.

Modern recipes are different, leaning toward the idea of rich pound or sponge cake layered with the ricotta-liqueur or sweet-wine filling. What has always been common to the cassata, however, is a ripening process using liqueur. The choice of spirit is essential to the cake's flavor.

In fact, many classic Italian cakes call for liqueur or sweet wines as ingredients. The Currant Sponge Cake or *Rasprato,* for example, is traditionally glazed with an apricot-brandy icing. And strawberries liberally bathed in Marsala and sugar are the distinctive ingredients behind the ring-shaped classic known as *Buccellato.*

In a filling or glaze, fresh fruit and jams are the favorite ingredients. A simple Italian pear cake or *Torte di Pere,* for instance, calls for fresh pears and pine nuts to be spooned into a rich cake batter. Other fruits and jams, such as fresh strawberries and strawberry jam, are fillings for a Strawberry Cream Sponge Cake or *Pan di Spagna con Crema di Fragole.* Other popular ingredients are the combined chocolate and espresso in a very rich, moist and creamy Chocolate-Espresso Cake, or *Torta al Cioccolato con Espresso.*

Because Italians draw from a wide variety of spices, sugars and spirits, some classics may be adapted into lowered-fat, but tempting, slices of torta heaven, such as the Chocolate Pistachio *(Torta al Cioccolato con Pistacchio)* and Lemon-Anise Sponge *(Torta di Limone e Anice)*. Both are perfect summer desserts when served with a bowl of fresh fruit.

Sicilian Cassata

*C*assata, symbolizing rebirth, is a cake served for birthdays, weddings and Easter. Amaretto is the perfect spirit for the ripening.

Cake:

1/2 cup butter, room temperature

1 cup granulated sugar

1/2 cup milk

3 egg yolks, well beaten

1/2 teaspoon vanilla extract

1/8 teaspoon mace

1-1/2 tablespoons lemon zest

2 cups cake flour

1/4 teaspoon cream of tartar

1/4 teaspoon salt

Filling:

1 (15-oz.) container ricotta cheese

1-1/2 tablespoons half-and-half

1/4 cup powdered sugar

1/4 cup shredded coconut

3 tablespoons Amaretto

1/2 cup semisweet chocolate chips

Semisweet Chocolate Frosting:

1-1/2 cups semisweet chocolate chips

3/4 cup brewed espresso or strong black coffee

1/2 lb. chilled butter, cut into thin slices

Preheat oven to 350F (180C). Coat a 9 x 5-inch loaf pan with vegetable-oil spray and flour. In a large bowl, using an electric mixer, beat 1/2 cup butter and granulated sugar. Add milk, beaten egg yolks, vanilla, mace and lemon zest and mix until creamy. Gradually beat in cake flour, cream of tartar and salt; then pour and spread evenly into prepared loaf pan.

Bake for 50 minutes or until wooden pick inserted into center comes out clean. Cool 20 minutes; then invert onto rack to cool.

To Prepare Filling: In a large bowl, using an electric mixer whip ricotta cheese, half-and-half, powdered sugar, coconut and Amaretto until smooth.

To Assemble Cassata: Using a serrated knife, slice the top, bottom and the two end crusts off cooled cake. Cut the cake horizontally into three even layers. On bottom layer, spoon one half of ricotta filling.

Carefully place next layer of cake on top, making certain sides and edges are even. Spread with more ricotta, repeat with next layer and filling until ending with a plain slice of cake on top. Gently press the layers together making them slightly compact. Cover loosely with waxed paper; refrigerate 4 hours to "ripen."

To Prepare Semisweet Chocolate Frosting: A few minutes before serving, melt semisweet chocolate chips with espresso or black coffee in a saucepan over low heat, stirring constantly until chocolate dissolves. Remove pan from heat. Using an electric mixer, beat in 1/2 lb. butter, 1 slice at a time. Continue beating until mixture is smooth. Refrigerate frosting until it thickens to a spreading consistency.

Just prior to serving, use a small metal spatula to spread frosting evenly over the top, sides and ends of cake, making decorative swirls.

Makes 12 servings.

Date-Walnut Cassata

Cassata con Datteri e Noci

Ricotta cream, dates and walnuts are spread on two layers of a very light sponge cake flavored with anise and orange zest. As with any cassata, it is best served after ripening at least 4 hours in a refrigerator—or even overnight.

Cake:

2 whole eggs, separated

4 egg whites

3/4 cup plus 2 tablespoons granulated sugar

1 cup cake flour

1 teaspoon anise seed

3 tablespoons orange zest (1 medium orange)

1/2 cup whole milk or lowfat milk

1/2 teaspoon vanilla extract

1/8 teaspoon cream of tartar

Filling:

1 (15-oz.) container ricotta cheese

1 (3-oz) package cream cheese, room temperature

1-1/2 teaspoons Cointreau liqueur

1 cup powdered sugar

1 cup chopped dates

1/2 cup coarsely chopped walnuts

Preheat oven to 350F (180C). Coat a 13 x 9-inch baking pan with veg-etable-oil spray. In a large bowl, using an electric mixer, beat 2 egg yolks with 3/4 cup of sugar, reserving the remaining 6 egg whites and 2 tablespoons of sugar for later. Add cake flour, anise seed and orange zest; then pour in milk and vanilla and continue mixing until well blended. Set aside.

In another large bowl, whip reserved egg whites with 2 tablespoons reserved granulated sugar and cream of tartar until stiff peaks form. Gently fold meringue into cake mixture with rubber spatula; then pour evenly into prepared baking pan.

Bake on bottom rack of oven for 12 to 14 minutes or until tooth-pick inserted into center comes out clean. Remove from oven; then immediately loosen cake from edges of pan and invert onto rack to cool completely. If cake doesn't automatically loosen, use a sharp knife to gently pry the cake away from pan.

To Prepare Ricotta Filling: In large bowl, beat ricotta cheese, cream cheese, Cointreau and powdered sugar with an electric mixer until smooth; add dates and walnuts until well blended.

To Assemble Cake: When cake is completely cooled, using a serrat-ed knife cut into two equal portions. Place bottom layer on a serving platter. Carefully spread one half of ricotta filling evenly on bottom layer. Slide top layer onto cake and spread with remaining ricotta frost-ing. Cover loosely with waxed paper; refrigerate 4 hours for cassata to "ripen."

Makes 12 servings.

Strawberry Cream Sponge Cakes

Pan di Spagna con Crema di Fragole

*T*his classic sponge cake recipe from Naples is good with any rich cream-and-jam filling. My version is layered with strawberry jam and a rich cream made with fresh strawberries.

Cake:

5 whole eggs, separated

3/4 cup plus 2 tablespoons granulated sugar

1 cup cake flour

3 teaspoons baking powder

1/4 cup milk

1 teaspoon vanilla extract

Pinch of cream of tartar

Cream Filling:

1 cup whipping cream

1-1/2 tablespoons powdered sugar

1 cup fresh or frozen (well-drained) strawberries, sliced

Strawberry Glaze:

1/2 cup strawberry jam or preserves mixed with
    1 tablespoon lemon zest

Whole strawberries for garnish

Preheat oven to 350 degrees (180C). Liberally coat two 8-inch-round cake pans with vegetable-oil spray and flour.

In a large bowl using an electric mixer, beat egg yolks with 3/4 cup granulated sugar, (reserving the 5 egg whites and 2 tablespoons of sugar for later). Add cake flour and baking powder; then pour in milk and vanilla and continue mixing until well blended. Set aside.

In another large bowl, whip egg whites with the remaining 2 tablespoons sugar and cream of tartar until stiff peaks form. Gently fold meringue into cake mixture with rubber spatula; then pour and spread evenly in prepared baking pans.

Bake layers for 12 minutes or until wooden pick inserted into centers comes out clean. Remove both pans from oven; immediately loosen cakes from edges of pans and invert onto rack to cool. If cakes don't automatically loosen, use a sharp knife to pry the cake away from pans—very gently.

To Prepare Cream Filling: Using an electric mixer, whip cream and powdered sugar until stiff peaks form. Then gradually fold in strawberries with a rubber spatula.

To Assemble Cake: When sponge cakes are completely cooled, spread one layer with one half portion of strawberry-jam glaze; then with one half of strawberry-cream filling. Repeat with second sponge-cake layer, top with remaining portions of strawberry jam; then cream filling. Top with fresh, whole strawberries if desired.

Cover and refrigerate until ready to serve.

Makes 8-10 servings.

Currant Sponge Cake
Rasprato

A Neopolitan classic rich sponge cake filled with currants, apricot brandy and lemon rind makes an elegant dessert.

Cake:

1 cup butter, room temperature

1 cup granulated sugar

5 whole eggs

3-1/2 cups cake flour

3 teaspoons baking powder

1/2 teaspoon salt

1 cup of milk

1 teaspoon lemon zest

2 teaspoons apricot brandy

1/2 cup dried currants

Apricot Brandy Icing:

2 tablespoons butter

2-1/2 tablespoons milk

2 tablespoons apricot brandy

1 cup powdered sugar

2 tablespoons dried currants

Preheat oven to 350F (180C). Liberally coat a Bundt pan with vegetable-oil spray and flour. In a large bowl, with an electric mixer, beat 1 cup butter and granulated sugar until creamy. Beat in whole eggs one at a time until creamy. Gradually beat in dry ingredients (cake flour, baking powder and salt) in thirds, alternating with milk. Add lemon zest, apricot brandy and 1/2 cup currants; then pour and spread evenly in prepared Bundt pan.

Bake 40-45 minutes or until a wooden pick inserted comes out clean. Cool 20 minutes; then invert cake out of Bundt pan onto rack to cool completely.

To Prepare Icing: In a small saucepan, melt 2 tablespoons butter into milk over medium heat. Add apricot brandy; then whisk in powdered sugar. Stir in 2 tablespoons currants. Then increase heat and continue stirring until mixture comes to a slight boil.

Remove icing from heat and set aside to cool for 15 minutes. Place a sheet of waxed paper underneath the cake to catch dripped icing. Spoon icing over completely cooled cake.

Makes 8-9 servings.

Chocolate-Pistachio Cake
Torta al Cioccolato con Pistacchio

*T*his dainty chocolate-pistachio sponge cake is meant to be eaten when you want your dolci light, or dolci leggeri. Just a slice accompanied with fresh, summer fruit is low in fat, wonderful and perfect for chocolate-pistachio lovers.

Cake:

2 whole eggs, separated

3 egg whites

3/4 cup plus 2 tablespoons granulated sugar

1 cup cake flour

3 teaspoons baking powder

3 tablespoons unsweetened cocoa powder

1/2 cup lowfat milk

1 teaspoon vanilla

1/3 cup coarsely chopped pistachios

1/8 teaspoon cream of tartar

Topping:

1 to 2 tablespoons powdered sugar

Preheat oven to 350F (180C). Coat a 10-inch tube pan with vegetable-oil spray. In a large bowl, using an electric mixer, beat the 2 egg yolks with 3/4 cup sugar (reserving the 5 egg whites and remaining 2 tablespoons of sugar for later). Add cake flour, baking powder and cocoa powder; then pour in milk, vanilla and pistachios and continue mixing until well blended. Set aside.

In another large bowl, whip reserved egg whites with the remaining 2 tablespoons of granulated sugar and cream of tartar until stiff peaks form. Gently fold meringue into cake mixture with a rubber spatula; then pour and spread evenly in prepared pan. Bake on bottom rack of oven 12 to 14 minutes or until a wooden pick inserted comes out clean. Remove from oven and allow to cool about 10 minutes; then gently invert the cake onto a rack. With your fingers, hold cake on both sides and carefully invert again so bottom of cake is cooling on rack. When cake is completely cooled, sift powdered sugar on top.

This cake is a bit smaller than average, but it looks and tastes great when served with a light espresso, coffee or tea.

Makes 8-9 servings.

Raisin-Coconut Cake
Torta con Uva Secca e Cocco

*A*n adaptation of another rich Neopolitan cake with raisins, nuts and coconut—plus a glaze of your favorite preserves.

Cake:

1 cup butter, room temperature

1 cup granulated sugar

5 whole eggs

1 cup shredded coconut

1 cup black raisins

1/2 cup fine walnut crumbs

3 cups cake flour

3 teaspoons baking powder

1/2 teaspoon salt

1 cup milk

Fruit Glaze:

1/3 cup butter

1/3 cup favorite fruit preserves

1 cup powdered sugar

1/2 teaspoon vanilla extract

3 tablespoons hot water

Preheat oven to 350F (180C). Liberally coat a Bundt pan with vegetable-oil spray and flour. In a large bowl, with an electric mixer beat 1 cup butter and granulated sugar. Add whole eggs one at a time, beating after each addition; then add coconut, raisins and walnuts and continue beating until thoroughly blended. Gradually add cake flour, baking powder and salt, alternating with milk in thirds.

Pour and spread cake evenly in prepared Bundt pan. Bake 40-45 minutes or until a wooden pick inserted in the out clean. Cool 20 minutes; then invert cake out of Bundt pan onto rack to cool for another 15 minutes before topping with glaze.

To Prepare Fruit Glaze: Melt 1/3 cup butter into preserves in a medium-size saucepan over medium heat. Gradually whisk in powdered sugar and vanilla until thoroughly blended. Stir in water, 1 tablespoon at a time, until glaze is smooth and syrupy. Remove from heat and cool slightly; then place a sheet of wax paper directly under cake rack. Spoon warm glaze on top and sides of cake until cake is completely bathed. Allow to cool for at least 1-1/2 to 2 hours before serving.

Makes 8-9 servings.

Strawberry-Marsala Cake
Buccellato

A buccellato, from the Ligurian province of La Spezia, is a classic, angel-light, raisin-anise cake centered with a ring of fresh, sliced strawberries bathed in Marsala. Perfect for creating summer colors or sweet impressions.

Strawberry Bath:

1 cup fresh strawberries, sliced

1/2 cup Marsala

1/3 cup granulated sugar

Cake:

12 egg whites

1 teaspoon cream of tartar

1/2 cup granulated sugar

1 teaspoon vanilla extract

1-1/4 cups cake flour

1/8 teaspoon salt

1 cup raisins

2 teaspoons anise seeds, lightly crushed

Marsala Icing:

1/3 cup butter

2 cups powdered sugar

2 tablespoons hot water

Preheat oven to 350F (180C). You will need a 10-inch ungreased tube pan with a removable rim. Soak sliced strawberries in 1/2 cup Marsala and 1/3 cup sugar. Set aside to chill in refrigerator. In a large mixing bowl, beat egg whites with cream of tartar until stiff enough to form soft peaks but still moist and glossy. Add 1/2 cup granulated sugar, 2 tablespoons at a time, and vanilla, continuing to beat until egg whites hold stiff peaks.

With a rubber spatula, gently fold in cake flour mixed with 1/8 teaspoon salt, alternately in thirds. While folding in final third of flour, add raisins and lightly crushed anise seed. Do not overstir or the batter will lose its foamy consistency. Pour and spread evenly into a ungreased tube pan, gently sliding the rubber spatula over the top to release any air bubbles. Bake on bottom rack of oven for 30 minutes or until top is light golden and cake springs back when touched.

Remove cake from oven and allow to cool slightly; then invert the cake in pan over the neck of a bottle as a handy stand. Let cake stand upside down on the bottle for about 1-1/2 hours until completely cooled. Gently slip a knife along the insides and funnel of pan. Lift the removable rim and use the knife to separate the cake from the rim. Cover the cake with your serving platter and invert cake from pan.

To Assemble Cake: Drain Marsala from strawberries, reserving 2 tablespoons of liquid for icing.

When cake has completely cooled, melt butter and reserved 2 tablespoons of Marsala over medium heat. Whisk in powdered sugar; stir in water 1 tablespoon at a time until smooth and syrupy. Remove from heat and cool slightly; then spread warm icing over cake

Spoon sugared strawberries into the center funnel of the angel cake just before serving. Serve spoonfuls of sugared strawberries over cake slices when serving.

Makes 10-12 servings.

Orange-Chocolate Easter Cake
Torta di Pasqua

Torta di Pasqua means an Easter cake. And Easter Sunday meant an array of orange-chiffon cakes filled with ricotta fillings. This cassata is layered with ricotta, orange zest and semisweet chocolate chips.

Cake:
2-1/4 cups cake flour

1-1/2 cups granulated sugar

3 teaspoons baking powder

1 teaspoon salt

3/4 cup orange juice

1/2 cup canola oil

1/2 teaspoon vanilla extract

2 teaspoons orange zest

6 egg yolks, well beaten

1 cup egg whites (about 8)

1/2 teaspoon cream of tartar

Ricotta Filling:
1 (15-oz.) container ricotta cheese

1 (3-oz.) package cream cheese, room temperature

2 teaspoons orange zest

1 cup powdered sugar

1 teaspoon vanilla extract

1/4 cup semisweet chocolate drops

Vanilla Glaze:
1/3 cup butter

2 cups powdered sugar

1 teaspoon vanilla extract

2-1/2 to 3 tablespoons hot water

Topping:

1/4 cup ground nuts, divided

Preheat oven to 325F (160C). Coat a 10-inch tube pan with vegetable-oil spray. In a large bowl, mix cake flour, granulated sugar, baking powder and salt. With an electric mixer beat in orange juice, canola oil, vanilla, orange zest and beaten egg yolks until mixture is smooth. In another large bowl, with an electric mixer, beat egg whites and cream of tartar until stiff peaks form. Using a rubber spatula, carefully fold in cake-and-egg-yolk mixture into meringue just until blended. Pour and spread evenly in ungreased tube pan.

Bake 1 hour and 5 minutes on bottom rack of oven, or until top of cake springs back when touched. Remove cake from oven and allow to cool for 10 minutes. Immediately invert tube pan onto rack to loosen cake from pan. Cool completely.

To Prepare Ricotta Filling: In large bowl, using an electric mixer beat ricotta cheese, cream cheese, orange zest, 1 cup powdered sugar and vanilla until smooth. Turn off mixer. With a wooden spoon stir semisweet chocolate chips into filling. Cover and refrigerate until ready to assemble cake.

To Prepare Vanilla Glaze: In a medium saucepan heat butter until melted. Whisk in 2 cups powdered sugar and vanilla; stir in hot water, 1 tablespoon at a time until smooth and syrupy. Remove from heat and cool to lukewarm before assembling cake.

To Assemble Cake: When cake has completely cooled, using a long serrated knife, slice cake in half to create a two-layer tiered cake. Place bottom layer on serving platter. Using a rubber spatula, gently spread filling over first layer. Sprinkle half of ground nuts on top of filling. Slide top layer onto cake and spread with lukewarm vanilla glaze and remaining nuts.

Makes 10-12 servings.

Ferrarese Chocolate Cake
Torta al Cioccolato alla Ferrarese

Ferrarese Cioccolato Torta is a divine chocolate-cinnamon cake frosted with meringue, topped with chocolate-covered almonds.

Cake:

2 cups plus 2 tablespoons cake flour

2/3 cup unsweetened cocoa, sifted

1-1/2 cups granulated sugar

3 teaspoons baking powder

1 teaspoon salt

1 teaspoon ground cinnamon

1/2 cup cold water

2/3 cup canola oil

6 egg yolks, well beaten

2 teaspoons lemon zest

1 cup egg whites (about 8)

1/2 teaspoon cream of tartar

Meringue:

1/4 cup white corn syrup

1/2 cup granulated sugar

2 tablespoons water

2 egg whites

1 teaspoon vanilla extract

Garnish:

2 tablespoons lemon zest

12 whole chocolate-covered almonds for garnish

Preheat oven to 325F (160C). Coat a 10-inch tube pan with vegetable-oil spray. In a large bowl, using an electric mixer, mix cake flour, sifted cocoa, 1-1/2 cups granulated sugar, baking powder, salt, cinnamon, cold water, canola oil, beaten egg yolks and lemon zest until smooth and creamy.

In another large bowl, with an electric mixer beat 1 cup egg whites and cream of tartar until stiff peaks form. Using a rubber spatula, carefully fold cake mixture into meringue until just blended. Pour into prepared tube pan. Bake on lower rack of oven 55 to 60 minutes, or until top of cake springs back when touched. Remove cake from oven and cool for 10 minutes. Immediately invert pan onto rack to loosen cake from pan. Cool completely.

To Prepare Meringue: Combine corn syrup, 1/2 cup granulated sugar and water in a medium-size saucepan. Cover and bring to a boil over medium heat; then reduce heat to low and simmer 5 to 7 minutes, without stirring, to 242F (117C) on candy thermometer. Mixture will be syrupy.

In a large bowl, with an electric mixer beat 2 egg whites until stiff peaks form; then pour corn syrup mixture gradually into egg whites while beating continuously on medium speed. Add vanilla. Increase speed to high; continue beating 10 minutes until stiff peaks form.

To Assemble Cake: When cake has cooled, use a long serrated knife to slice cake in half to create a two-layer tiered cake. Place bottom layer on serving platter. Using a rubber spatula, gently spread one half portion of meringue over bottom layer. **Don't cover sides!** Slide top layer onto cake and top with remaining meringue, lemon zest and 12 chocolate-covered almonds (one for each serving) around the cake.

Makes 12 servings.

Lemon Anise Cake

Torta di Limone e Anice

*T*his very light, lemon-anise sponge cake is very simple and easy to prepare.

Cake:

2 whole eggs, separated

4 egg whites

3/4 cup plus 2 tablespoons granulated sugar

1 cup cake flour

1 tablespoon baking powder

1/2 teaspoon anise seed

3 tablespoons lemon zest

1/2 cup whole milk or lowfat milk

1 teaspoon vanilla extract

1/8 teaspoon cream of tartar

Glaze:

1 tablespoon butter

1 tablespoon lemon juice

1 cup powdered sugar

Preheat oven to 350F (180C). Coat a 10-inch tube pan with vegetable-oil spray. In a large bowl, with an electric mixer beat 2 egg yolks and 3/4 cup granulated sugar (reserving remaining 6 egg whites and remaining 2 tablespoons sugar for later). Add cake flour, baking powder, anise seed and lemon zest; pour in milk and vanilla. Set aside.

In another large bowl, with an electric mixer whip the 6 egg whites with the remaining 2 tablespoons of granulated sugar and cream of tartar until stiff peaks form. Gently fold meringue into cake mixture with a rubber spatula; then pour and spread mixture evenly in prepared tube pan.

Bake on bottom rack of oven for 15 minutes or until a toothpick inserted comes out clean. Remove from oven and allow to cool for about 5 minutes; then gently invert the pan onto rack to loosen cake from pan; cool completely.

To Prepare Glaze:　When cake is completely cooled, make glaze. In a small saucepan over medium heat, melt butter into lemon juice. Whisk in powdered sugar until glaze is smooth. Remove from heat and cool slightly.

Place a sheet of wax paper under cake rack. Then brush warm glaze over surface of cake.

Makes 10-12 servings.

Pear Pound Cake
Torta di Pere

*T*his rich coconut pound-cake recipe was inspired by my mother who, like most Italians, loved mixing fresh fruit into cake batters.

Pear Filling:

2 teaspoons butter

1 tablespoon brown sugar

1/4 teaspoon vanilla extract

1 pear, quartered, cored, and thinly sliced with peel

1/4 teaspoon ground cinnamon

1/4 cup pine nuts

Cake:

3 cups cake flour

1 teaspoon baking powder

1/8 teaspoon salt

1/2 teaspoon ground nutmeg

1 cup flaked coconut

2-1/2 cups granulated sugar

1 cup butter, room temperature

4 whole eggs

2 tablespoons lemon juice

3/4 cup milk

Lemon Glaze:

1/3 cup lemon juice

3/4 cup and 1 tablespoon granulated sugar

Preheat oven to 350F (180F). Coat a Bundt pan with vegetable-oil spray and flour.

In a saucepan over medium heat, melt butter into brown sugar and vanilla. Add sliced unpeeled pear, cinnamon and pine nuts. Cook while stirring until pear slices are translucent and pine nuts are golden. Remove from heat; set aside.

In a large bowl, mix cake flour, baking powder, salt, nutmeg and flaked coconut with a fork until blended; set aside. In another large mixing bowl, with an electric mixer beat 2-1/2 cups granulated sugar, butter and eggs (one at a time). Add dry ingredients alternately in thirds with lemon juice and milk. Continue mixing until ingredients are thoroughly blended in a thick batter. Pour and spread half of batter evenly in prepared Bundt pan. Then carefully spoon in the pear filling. Cover pear filling with the remaining batter.

Bake 1 hour or until a wooden pick inserted comes out clean. Cool 20 minutes; then invert cake out of Bundt pan and onto rack. Immediately brush Lemon Glaze over cake.

To Prepare Lemon Glaze: In a medium bowl, whisk lemon juice and 3/4 cup sugar, reserving the remaining 1 tablespoon of sugar for later; continue whisking until frothy. Brush glaze over the entire surface of partially cooled cake; then sift reserved 1 tablespoon of granulated sugar evenly over cake. Cool glazed cake completely on rack before serving.

Makes 8-9 servings.

Chocolate-Espresso Cake
Torta al Cioccolato con Espresso

*C*ombining espresso and chocolate makes a heavenly dense cake.

Cake:

1-1/2 cups semisweet chocolate chips

1/2 cup butter

3/4 cup cake flour

4 whole eggs, separated

1/2 cup granulated sugar

1/8 teaspoon cream of tartar

Chocolate-Espresso Glaze:

1/2 cup semisweet chocolate chips

2 tablespoons butter

2 tablespoons brewed espresso or strong coffee

2 tablespoons corn syrup

1/3 cup slivered almonds for topping

Pre-heat oven to 325F (160C). Liberally coat a 9-inch round springform cake pan (with removable bottom) with vegetable-oil spray. In a medium-size saucepan over medium heat, melt 1-1/2 cups chocolate chips and 1/2 cup butter. Remove from heat and cool until chocolate mixture is lukewarm. In a large bowl, with an electric mixer mix cooled chocolate mixture, cake flour, and 4 egg yolks (reserving 4 whites for later) until ingredients are well blended.

In another large bowl, beat remaining egg whites on high speed until foamy. Beat in granulated sugar, 1 tablespoon at a time, and cream of tartar until soft peaks form. Gently fold chocolate cake mixture into beaten egg whites with a rubber spatula until blended. Spread cake mixture evenly in springform pan.

Bake 40 minutes or until wooden pick inserted into center comes out clean. Remove from oven and cool 10 minutes; then run a knife along cake sides to loosen; then remove side of springform pan. Invert cake onto rack; remove bottom disk.

To Prepare Glaze: When cake is completely cooled, invert again onto serving platter. In a small saucepan, heat 1/2 cup chocolate chips with 2 tablespoons butter, espresso or coffee and corn syrup over medium heat, stirring constantly until chips are melted. Continue stirring until mixture comes to a boil and coats the rounded edge of spoon, about 3 minutes. Using a rubber spatula, spread hot sauce over cake allowing excess to drizzle down sides. Top with slivered almonds and serve.

Makes 10-12 servings.

Tarts

Crostate

❦❦❦❦❦❦❦

*C*rostate are desserts with pastry. *Pasta frolla* means pastry that covers a wide array of fruit and cheese fillings. Compared to American pie crust, pasta frolla is less flaky, a bit more crumbly, and typically richer in flavor with ingredients such as orange or lemon zest, sweet wine or anise seed.

To obtain richness in pasta frolla, butter was traditionally the favored shortening in Northern Italy, particularly in the pastures of Piedmont and Lombardy. Olive oil is the Southerner's choice because of its abundance, and because for many Southern Italian farmers, raising cattle was a luxury.

Today, however, many Italians are opting for a shortening with less saturated fat, particularly canola oil. While I experimented with different shortenings and amounts, I found that mixing canola oil with a small amount of butter yields a most desirable flavor and crumble. And canola oil contains far less saturated fat than all-butter shortenings, hydrogenated vegetable shortenings or lard.

Blending and Shaping Pasta Frolla

Perhaps the biggest rule is: never overwork dough while blending ingredients, either by hand or by electric mixer, or the pastry will become tough and difficult to handle. When pouring liquids into pastry ingredients, pour one spoonful at a time.

To shape pasta frolla, press the dough into a ball, wrap it in foil or plastic wrap and refrigerate for the time indicated in each recipe. The higher the shortening content is in relation to the other ingredients, the longer the pastry dough should be refrigerated.

Start by flattening the center of the dough with a rolling pin. Using even pressure, start from the center and roll to the far edges until dough is about 1/8 inch thick. Take care to use as little flour as possible when rolling or shaping dough. Too much flour alters the proportion and texture.

Baking Tarts or Crostate

A 9-inch tart pan works best for smaller custard or cheese tarts; the same size pan with a removable side rim and bottom disk is preferred when a filling calls for rows of fresh fruit. Springform cake pans with removable bottom disks work best for almost any deep-dish tart.

Baking "Blind"

Some deep-dish tarts with chilled cream, lots of fruit or fresh fruit, may call for a pastry-baking method known as "baking blind." This is easily done by piercing the unbaked tart shells at close intervals with a fork before baking to prevent the pastry from rising. Then loosely line the shell with foil or parchment paper and fill with dried beans or rice. The tart shell is typically baked for 10 minutes; then the foil or paper, beans or rice are removed and pastry is returned to oven for another 5 to 7 minutes. Allow for slight time variations on each recipe.

Fresh Fruit Tart

Crostata di Frutta Fresca

*F*resh fruit artfully arranged over a tart shell with an intriguing hint of anise, a truly beautiful presentation.

Tart Shell or Pasta Frolla:

1-1/3 cups all-purpose flour

1/2 cup granulated sugar

1/2 teaspoon anise seed

2 tablespoons cold butter, cut into small pieces

3 tablespoons canola oil

1 egg

1 tablespoon whipping cream or half-and-half

Fruit Jam and Fresh Fruit Filling:

1/4 cup raspberry jam

1-1/2 to 2 pints fresh raspberries or blueberries
   or combinations of both

4 kiwis, peeled and sliced

1 tablespoon honey

1 (11-oz) can mandarin oranges, drained, for garnish

Whipped cream or Vanilla Gelato

In a large bowl, combine flour, sugar and anise seed. Using a pastry cutter or two knives, cut butter and oil into dry ingredients until mixture is evenly distributed and becomes slightly crumbly (or use the paddle attachment of an electric mixer set at low speed). Make a well in the center and add egg and whipping cream or half-and-half.

Continue mixing until dough clings together. If needed to hold dough together, add 1 to 2 teaspoons of cold water. Gather dough into a mound and wrap in foil or plastic wrap. Place in refrigerator and chill 20 minutes.

Preheat oven to 350F (180C). You will need a 9-inch tart pan with a removable side rim and bottom disk.

Remove dough from refrigerator. On a lightly floured surface, roll out dough to fit tart pan. Transfer dough to tart pan, pressing with fingertips to fit bottom and sides. Then pierce sides and bottom with a fork. Line shell with foil or parchment paper and fill with dried beans or rice. Bake for 10 minutes. Remove foil or paper, beans or rice; return to oven at same temperature for 5 to 7 minutes or until golden brown. Cool slightly in pan; carefully lift tart by its removable bottom disk to release from side rim. Place on rack to cool.

To Assemble Tart or Crostata:　When tart shell is completely cooled, carefully remove the bottom disk from the tart shell using thumbs and fingertips. Place shell on serving platter. Then spoon jam onto bottom crust, but not sides. Starting with raspberries or blueberries, place one-third of berries in a center row of cooled tart shell. Next to the center row of berries, create two rows of sliced kiwi fruit; then on each end of tart shell, fill with the remaining berries. Drizzle honey over berries and kiwi; then garnish with mandarin orange slices.

Serve with whipped cream or Vanilla Gelato.

Makes 8-10 servings.

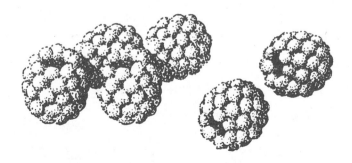

Ricotta and Raspberry Tart
Crostata di Ricotta e Lamponi

A Florentine tart calls for finely ground hazelnuts; the filling is a layer of cold, creamy ricotta and fresh raspberries.

Filling:
2 cups (1-1/2 lbs.) ricotta cheese

1/4 cup half-and-half

1/2 cup powdered sugar

1/2 teaspoon ground cinnamon

1 tablespoon orange zest

1/2 cup semisweet chocolate chips

Tart Shell or Pasta Frolla:
1 cup plus 2 tablespoons all-purpose flour

1/3 cup fine hazelnut or pecan crumbs

1/4 cup granulated sugar

1 teaspoon orange zest

2 tablespoons cold butter, cut into small pieces

5 tablespoons canola oil

1 egg

2 tablespoons cold water

Raspberry Topping:
2 pints fresh or frozen raspberries, rinsed and well drained

3 tablespoons brown sugar

1 teaspoon honey

Optional Garnish:
Semisweet chocolate shavings

To Prepare Ricotta Filling: In a large bowl, using an electric mixer, whip ricotta cheese, half and half, powdered sugar, cinnamon and 1 tablespoon orange zest until mixture is smooth. Add chocolate chips; then spoon cheese mixture into a bowl and chill in refrigerator at least 2 hours before filling baked tart shell.

To Prepare Tart Shell: In another large bowl, combine flour, hazelnuts or pecans, granulated sugar and 1 teaspoon orange zest. Using a pastry blender or two knives, cut butter and oil into dry ingredients until mixture is evenly distributed and becomes slightly crumbly (or, use the paddle attachment of an electric mixer set at low speed). Make a well in the center and add egg and cold water and continue mixing until dough clings together. If needed, add 1 to 2 teaspoons of cold water to hold dough together. Gather dough into a mound and wrap in foil or plastic wrap. Place in refrigerator and allow to chill 20 minutes.

Preheat oven to 350F (180C). You will need a 9-inch tart pan. Remove dough from refrigerator. On a lightly floured surface, roll out dough to fit tart pan. Transfer dough to pan, pressing with fingertips to fill bottom and sides. Then pierce sides and bottom of shell with a fork. Line shell with foil or parchment paper and fill with dried beans or rice.

Bake for 10 minutes. Remove foil or paper, beans or rice; return to oven at same temperature for 5 to 7 minutes or until golden brown. Remove from oven. Set aside to cool.

To Fill Tart or Crostata: In a large bowl, carefully mix raspberries with brown sugar and honey until coated. Refrigerate.

To Assemble Crostata: When tart shell is completely cooled, remove chilled ricotta filling from refrigerator. Spoon an even layer of chilled ricotta mixture inside shell. Spread the raspberry topping over the filling. Garnish with semisweet chocolate shavings if desired. Loosely cover with plastic wrap or waxed paper and refrigerate until serving.

Makes 8-10 servings.

Pear-Rum Crostata (deep dish)
Crostata di Pere con Rum

*P*ears from the Ferrara area of Italy, especially around Tresigallo, or the William and Principe Alberto pears from the provinces of Emilia-Romagna, are favorite Italian fruits for tarts.

Tart Shell or Pasta Frolla:
2-1/2 cups all-purpose flour
1/2 cup granulated sugar
1 teaspoon lemon zest
2 tablespoons cold butter, cut into small pieces
3/4 cup canola oil
3 tablespoons cold water

Filling:
5 cups firm ripe pears, peeled, cored and
    cut into bite-size pieces (5 or 6 pears)
1/3 cup apricot jam
3-1/2 tablespoons brown sugar
1 teaspoon flour
1/2 teaspoon ground cinnamon
1/4 teaspoon ground cloves
3 teaspoons dark rum
1 teaspoon canola oil

Egg-White Glaze:
1 egg white
1 tablespoon water

Vanilla yogurt for garnish.

In a large bowl, combine 2-1/2 cups flour, granulated sugar and lemon zest. Using a pastry blender or 2 knives, cut butter and 3/4 cup oil into dry ingredients until mixture becomes slightly crumbly (or use the paddle attachment of an electric mixer set at low speed). Make a well in the center and pour in cold water. Continue mixing until dough clings together. If needed, add 1 to 2 teaspoons of cold water to hold dough together. Gather dough into a mound and wrap in foil or plastic wrap. Refrigerate at least 1 hour.

To Prepare Pear Filling: In a large bowl, using a wooden spoon, mix pears, apricot jam, brown sugar, 1 teaspoon flour, cinnamon, cloves, dark rum and   teaspoon canola oil until well blended. Set aside.

Remove dough from refrigerator. On a lightly floured surface, roll out three quarters of the dough to fit bottom and sides of a 9-inch springform cake pan, reserving the rest for later. Place dough in pan, pressing with fingertips to bottom and sides. Return unbaked tart shell to refrigerator; chill 20 minutes. Meanwhile, roll out remaining dough, cut into long, even strips about 1/2 inch wide; cover with foil or plastic wrap and refrigerate.

Preheat oven to 350F (180C). Pierce sides and bottom of chilled unbaked shell with a fork. Line with foil or parchment paper and fill with dried beans or rice. Bake for 10 minutes. Remove foil or paper, beans or rice; return to oven at same temperature for 5 minutes. Remove from oven and set aside to cool, about 10 minutes.

Increase oven temperature to 400F (200C). Pour and spread pear filling evenly over cooled tart shell.

In a cup, whip egg white with water to make a glaze. Arrange refrigerated dough strips over pear filling in a lattice pattern. Brush strips with egg-white glaze. Return to oven for 30 to 35 minutes or until top is golden brown. If pastry becomes too brown, loosely cover with foil.

Remove tart from oven and cool 5 minutes. Carefully remove the side rim of the springform cake pan, leaving bottom disk in place. Place on a rack to cool. When tart is completely cooled, about 1-1/2 to 2 hours, lift and slide the bottom crust from disk with a sharp knife or wide metal spatula. Serve with dollops of vanilla yogurt.

Makes 8-10 servings.

Apple Crostata (deep-dish)
Crostata di Mele

*T*his crostata moves to a lighter side, with less shortening in the tart shell. And instead of using flour or cornstarch thickeners for fruit fillings, Italians enrich them with fruit jams. Here apples are mixed with apricot jam, Marsala and spices in a sublime filling.

Tart Shell or Pasta Frolla:

2-1/2 cups all-purpose flour

1/4 cup granulated sugar

1/4 cup brown sugar

1 teaspoon lemon zest

2 tablespoons cold butter, cut into small pieces

1/2 cup canola oil

3 tablespoons Marsala

3 tablespoons lowfat milk

Filling:

5 cups green apples, peeled, cored
   and cut into bite-size pieces (about 6 apples)

1/3 cup apricot jam

3-1/2 tablespoons brown sugar

1 teaspoon flour

1/2 teaspoon ground cinnamon

1/4 teaspoon ground cloves

3 teaspoons Marsala

1 teaspoon canola oil

Egg-White Glaze:

1 egg white

1 tablespoon water

In a large bowl, combine 2-1/2 cups flour, granulated and brown sugars and lemon zest. Using a pastry blender or 2 knives, cut butter and oil into dry ingredients until mixture is evenly distributed and crumbly (or use the paddle attachment of an electric mixer set at low speed). Make a well in the center; pour in 3 tablespoons Marsala and milk. Continue mixing until dough clings together. If needed, add 1 to 2 teaspoons of cold water to hold dough together. Gather dough into a mound and wrap in foil or plastic wrap. Refrigerator and allow to chill 40 minutes.

To Prepare Apple Filling: In a large bowl, using a wooden spoon, mix apples, apricot jam, brown sugar, 1 teaspoon flour, cinnamon, cloves, 3 teaspoons Marsala and 1 teaspoon canola oil until blended. Set aside.

Remove dough from refrigerator. On a lightly floured surface, roll out three quarters of the dough to fit bottom and sides of a 9-inch springform cake pan with a removable bottom disk, reserving the rest for later. Place dough in pan, pressing with fingertips to fit bottom and sides. Refrigerate unbaked for 30 minutes. Roll out remaining dough, cut into long, even strips about 1/2 inch wide; cover with foil or plastic wrap and refrigerate.

Preheat oven to 350F (180C). Pierce sides and bottom of chilled unbaked shell with a fork. Line with foil or parchment paper and fill with dried beans or rice. Bake 10 minutes. Remove foil or paper, beans or rice; return to oven at same temperature for 5 minutes. Remove from oven and set aside to cool about 10 minutes.

Increase oven temperature to 400F (200C). Pour and spread apple filling over tart shell.

In a cup, whip egg white with water to make a glaze. Arrange refrigerated dough strips over apple filling in a lattice pattern. Brush strips with egg-white glaze. Return tart to oven 30-35 minutes longer or until golden brown. If pastry becomes too brown, cover loosely with foil.

Remove tart from oven and cool about 5 minutes. Carefully remove side rim of springform pan, leaving the bottom disk in place. Place on a rack to cool. When tart is completely cooled, about 1-1/2 to 2 hours, lift and slide the bottom crust from disk with a sharp knife and wide metal spatula.

Makes 8-10 servings.

Ricotta Crostata *(deep dish)*
Crostata di Ricotta

*T*his recipe is based on the ancient Roman cheesecake recipe that used a fresh-crushed cheese similar to ricotta. Traditionally, Crostata di Ricotta was baked in an oven under an earthenware cover.

Tart Shell or Pasta Frolla:
2-1/2 cups all-purpose flour
1/4 cup granulated sugar
1/4 cup brown sugar
1 teaspoon lemon zest
2 tablespoons cold butter, cut into small pieces
3/4 cup canola oil
3-1/2 tablespoons Marsala

Filling:
5 cups ricotta cheese
1/2 cup powdered sugar
1 tablespoon all-purpose flour
1 teaspoon ground cinnamon
1/4 cup diced citron
1/4 cup golden raisins
3 tablespoons coarsely chopped walnuts
3 tablespoons flaked coconut
2 tablespoons pine nuts
1 tablespoon lemon zest
1 teaspoon vanilla extract

Egg-White Glaze:
1 egg white
1 tablespoon water

Powdered sugar for garnish

To Prepare Tart Shell: In a large bowl, combine 2-1/2 cups flour, granulated and brown sugars and 1 teaspoon lemon zest. Using a pastry blender or two knives, cut butter and oil into dry ingredients until mixture is evenly distributed and becomes slightly crumbly (or use the paddle attachment of an electric mixer set at low speed). Make a well in the center and pour in Marsala. Continue mixing until dough clings together. If needed, add 1 to 2 teaspoons cold water to hold dough together. Gather dough into a mound; wrap in foil or plastic wrap. Chill.

Remove dough from refrigerator. On a lightly floured surface, roll out three quarters of the dough to fit bottom and sides of 9-inch springform cake pan, reserving the rest for later. Place dough in pan, pressing with fingertips to fit bottom and sides. Return unbaked tart shell to refrigerator; chill 20 minutes. Roll out remaining dough and cut into long, even strips about 1/2 inch wide. Cover with foil or plastic wrap and refrigerate.

Preheat oven to 350F (180C). Pierce sides and bottom of chilled unbaked shell with a fork. Line with foil or parchment paper, and fill with dried beans or rice. Bake 10 minutes. Remove foil or paper, beans or rice; return to oven at same temperature for 5 minutes. Remove from oven; cool about 10 minutes. Meanwhile start ricotta filling.

To Prepare Ricotta Filling: In a large bowl, using an electric mixer, whip ricotta cheese, powdered sugar, 1 tablespoon flour and cinnamon; add citron, golden raisins, walnuts, flaked coconut, pine nuts, 1 tablespoon lemon zest and vanilla; mix until smooth. Spoon ricotta filling into partially-baked tart shell, smoothing the top with a rubber spatula.

In a cup, whip egg white with water to make a glaze. Arrange refrigerated dough strips in a lattice pattern over cheese filling. Brush strips with egg-white glaze. Return to oven at 350F (180C) for 65 minutes or until crust is golden brown and filling is firm. If pastry becomes too brown, loosely cover top of crust with foil.

Remove from oven; cool 5 minutes. Carefully remove side rim of cake pan, leaving bottom disk. Place on a rack to cool, about 2 hours. Lift and slide crust from disk using a sharp knife and wide metal spatula.

Sprinkle with powdered sugar. Store covered in refrigerator.

Makes 8-10 servings.

Chocolate-Espresso Cream Tart
from Naples
Crostata alla' Napoletana

*W*hen Neopolitans create something, they do it "to the max," as in this classic tart's delectable filling.

Tart Shell or Pasta Frolla:

1-1/2 tablespoons all-purpose flour

1/3 cup powdered sugar

1 teaspoon lemon zest

2 tablespoons cold butter, cut into small pieces

1/3 cup canola oil

2 tablespoons cold water

Cream Filling:

1-1/2 tablespoons gelatin

1/4 cup cold water

2 oz. sweet chocolate

1/4 cup brewed espresso or strong coffee

3/4 cup milk

1/3 cup brown sugar

1/4 teaspoon salt

2 beaten egg yolks

1 teaspoon vanilla

1/2 teaspoon ground cinnamon

1 cup whipping cream

1/4 teaspoon cream of tartar

1/4 cup granulated sugar

1/4 cup apricot jam

Semisweet chocolate shavings for garnish

In a large bowl, combine flour, powdered sugar and lemon zest. Using a pastry blender or 2 knives, cut butter and oil into dry ingredients until mixture is evenly distributed and becomes slightly crumbly (or use the paddle attachment of an electric mixer set at low speed). Make a well in the center and pour in cold water. Continue mixing until dough clings together. Add 1 to 2 teaspoons cold water if needed to hold dough together. Gather dough into a mound and wrap in foil or plastic wrap. Refrigerate 20 minutes. Prepare chocolate-espresso cream.

To Prepare Chocolate-Espresso Cream: In a cup stir gelatin into 1/4 cup water. Set aside 5 minutes to soften. In a double boiler, melt sweet chocolate into espresso or coffee and milk over medium heat. Stir in brown sugar, salt, beaten egg yolks, vanilla and cinnamon. Continue stirring until creamy mixture heavily coats spoon. Stir in softened gelatin until well blended; then set aside to cool completely.

Preheat oven to 350F (180C). Remove dough from refrigerator. On a lightly floured surface, roll dough to fit a 9-inch tart pan. Place dough in pan, pressing with fingertips to fit bottom and sides. Pierce sides and bottom of shell with a fork. Line with foil or parchment paper and fill with dried beans or rice. Bake 10 minutes; remove foil or paper, beans or rice; return to oven at same temperature for 5 to 7 minutes or until crust is golden brown. Remove from oven and cool.

To Prepare Filling: In a large bowl, using an electric mixer, whip cream, cream of tartar and granulated sugar until stiff peaks hold. Using a rubber spatula, gently fold whipped-cream mixture into cooled chocolate mixture until thoroughly blended. Set aside in refrigerator.

To Assemble Tart or Crostata: When tart shell is completely cooled, spread a thin layer of apricot jam on bottom only, **not sides**, of crust. Next, using a rubber spatula, spread chilled chocolate-espresso cream smoothly and evenly. Cover loosely with foil or waxed paper. Refrigerate at least 4 hours or until ready to serve. Garnish with semi-sweet chocolate shavings.

Makes 8-10 servings.

Orange-Apple Tart *(deep dish)*
Crostata di Arance e Mele

*I*talians—particularly in the North—love combining fruit and creams in their tarts.

Tart Shell or Pasta Frolla:
2-1/2 cups all-purpose flour

1/2 cup granulated sugar

1 teaspoon lemon zest

2 tablespoons cold butter, cut into small pieces

3/4 cup canola oil

3-1/2 tablespoons cold water

Orange Cream:
3 egg yolks

1/2 cup powdered sugar

2 tablespoons flour

1-1/4 cups orange juice

1 teaspoon Amaretto liqueur

1 teaspoon orange zest

Apple-Amaretto Filling:
5 cups thinly sliced, pared, tart apples (4-6 apples)

1/4 cup granulated sugar

1 teaspoon brown sugar

1-1/2 tablespoons flour

1/2 cup raisins

2 tablespoons Amaretto liqueur

1 teaspoon canola oil

Egg-White Glaze:
1 egg white
1 tablespoon water

In a large bowl, combine 2-1/2 cups flour, 1/2 cup granulated sugar and lemon zest. Using a pastry blender or 2 knives, cut butter and 3/4 cup oil into dry ingredients until mixture is evenly distributed and becomes slightly crumbly (or use the paddle attachment of an electric mixer set at low speed). Make a well in the center and pour in cold water. Continue mixing until dough clings together. If needed, add 1 to 2 teaspoons of cold water to hold dough together. Gather dough into a mound and wrap in foil or plastic wrap. Place in refrigerator and allow to chill at least 1 hour.

To Prepare Orange Cream: In a large bowl, whisk egg yolks into powdered sugar, flour and orange juice until frothy and smooth. Pour mixture into a double boiler over medium heat and add 1 teaspoon Amaretto and orange zest. Continue stirring until cream coats spoon heavily. Set cream aside in refrigerator to cool completely.

To Prepare Apple-Amaretto Filling: In another large bowl, using a wooden spoon, mix sliced apples, 1/4 cup granulated sugar, brown sugar, 1-1/2 tablespoons flour, raisins, 2 tablespoons Amaretto and canola oil until well blended, then set aside. Remove dough from refrigerator. On a lightly floured surface, roll out three-quarters of the dough to fit the bottom and sides of a 9-inch springform cake pan with a removable bottom disk, reserving the rest for later. Place dough in pan, pressing with fingertips to fit bottom and sides. Return unbaked tart shell to refrigerator to chill for 30 minutes. Roll out remaining dough, cut into long, even strips about 1/2 inch wide; cover with foil or plastic wrap and refrigerate.

Preheat oven to 350F (180C). Pierce sides and bottom of chilled unbaked shell with a fork. Line with foil or parchment paper and fill

(Recipe continued on page 106)

with dried beans or rice. Bake 10 minutes. Remove foil or paper, beans or rice; return to oven at same temperature for 5 minutes. Remove from oven and set aside to cool about 10 minutes.

Increase oven temperature to 400F (200C).

To Assemble Tart or Crostata: Spread refrigerated orange cream over bottom of completely cooled tart shell. Then top with apple-Amaretto filling.

In a cup, whip egg white with water to make a glaze. Arrange refrigerated dough strips over apple filling in a lattice pattern. Brush strips with egg-white glaze. Bake 30 to 35 minutes longer or until golden brown. Cover with foil if pastry becomes too brown.

Remove tart from oven and cool slightly on a rack about 5 minutes. Carefully remove side rim of springform pan, leaving bottom disk in place. Place on a rack to cool, about 2 hours. Lift and slide bottom crust out from disk with a sharp knife and wide metal spatula.

Makes 8-10 servings.

Ice Creams and Fruit Ices
Gelati e Granite

From 1905 to 1917, my grandfather owned a gelateria and bicycle-rental shop on a busy corner of Vittoria and Emanuele Streets in Catania, Sicily. Each summer morning, the art of making lemon *granita* was performed under the watchful stare of my grandmother, Concetta Conti Siracusa.

Concetta was the youngest daughter of a baker known for his generosity in adding lots of fruit to his tarts and cakes. To maintain this reputation she had to be certain her workers were shaving enough bits of lemon peel into the ice. Otherwise she would be known as stingy, a stigma that could easily bring ruin upon her family's good name as merchants of sweet things to eat.

My mother's only interest in this daily ritual was to grab a cone of lemon granita and balance it with one hand while bicycling down to the shores of the Mediterranean for a cool swim. She took for granted her mother's art in concocting frozen desserts. This art was brought to the Sicilians by the Arabs who originally learned it from the Chinese.

By the time my grandparents were making and selling gelati and granite, Italy was well known for its fruit creams and ices. And my proud grandmother knew that the secret behind preparing them was to use fresh fruit and plenty of it.

That's why I've opted for adding lots of fresh fruit into my recipes for Italian creams and ices. Along with strawberries and raspberries, recipes for granite highlight some tropical fruits such as pineapple, and a combination of mango, peach and brown sugar for a rich-tasting pulp. There's also an ancient lemon granita made with enough freshly squeezed lemons and lemon zest to satisfy my grandmother. Serve *Granita di Mocha Latte* with brewed espresso, chocolate and cream, for a refreshingly different summer jolt.

Gelati Tips for Success

Measure all ingredients accurately.

Follow ice-cream maker manufacturer's instructions for adding ice and rock salt.

Before adding your cream mixture to the beaten egg yolks, make certain cream is at room temperature, or it will separate.

While cooking mixture of egg yolks and cream over low heat, be careful not to bring to a boil or the mixture will curdle and turn lumpy.

Vanilla Bean Gelato

Gelato alla Vaniglia

Gelati are far richer than American ice creams and served in a softer form. This basic vanilla gelato includes vanilla-bean-pod shavings.

> **3 cups whipping cream, room temperature**
>
> **2 teaspoons shredded vanilla bean
>   (3 to 4 inches of vanilla-bean pod)**
>
> **7 egg yolks**
>
> **1/2 cup sugar**

In a large saucepan, bring the whipping cream and shredded vanilla bean to a boil over low heat; remove from heat.

In a large bowl, beat egg yolks and sugar 3 minutes; slowly stir the vanilla-bean-and-cream mixture into the egg yolks until well blended. Return mixture to the saucepan and cook over very low heat, stirring constantly with a wooden spoon until mixture is thick enough to light-ly coat the spoon, about 5 minutes. Do not let the mixture boil or it will curdle and turn lumpy. Remove from heat and set mixture aside; cool to room temperature.

Pack a 2-quart ice-cream freezer with layers of cracked ice and coarse rock salt as recommended by the freezer manufacturer. Pour cooled mixture into the ice-cream can. Cover.

Turn electric ice-cream maker on and churn about 50 minutes or until motor slows or stops. If using a hand ice-cream maker, let stand 3 to 4 minutes before turning handle. Do not stop churning until gela-to becomes solid or mixture will turn lumpy.

To harden or ripen the gelato, scrape mixture from sides of can toward the bottom, place a piece of plastic wrap on the surface, and cover tightly. Place in freezer 2 hours.

Makes about 2 pints.

Neopolitan Strawberry Gelato
Gelato di Fragole alla Napoletana

*L*emon is added for tartness in this very rich classic recipe.

3 cups whipping cream, room temperature

1 pint fresh strawberries, halved, about 2 cups

8 egg yolks

1/2 cup sugar

1-1/2 teaspoons vanilla extract

1 tablespoon lemon zest

In a large saucepan, bring the whipping cream and halved strawberries to a boil over low heat; remove from heat. In a large bowl, beat egg yolks, sugar, vanilla and lemon zest 3 minutes; then stir the cream-strawberry mixture into egg yolks, stirring until blended. Return to the saucepan and cook over very low heat, stirring constantly with a wooden spoon until mixture is thick enough to lightly coat the spoon, about 5 minutes. Do not let the mixture boil or it will curdle and turn lumpy. Remove from heat and cool to room temperature.

Pack a 2-quart ice-cream freezer with layers of cracked ice and coarse rock salt in proportions recommended by the freezer manufacturer. Add cold water if advised by manufacturer. Pour the completely cooled mixture into the ice-cream can. Cover.

Turn electric ice-cream maker on and churn about 50 minutes or until motor slows or stops. If using a hand ice-cream maker, let stand for 3 to 4 minutes before turning handle. Do not stop churning until gelato becomes solid or mixture will turn lumpy.

To harden or ripen the gelato, scrape mixture from sides of can toward the bottom, place a piece of plastic wrap on the surface, and cover tightly. Place in freezer for 2 hours.

Makes about 2 pints.

Strawberry Ice

Granita di Fragole

*F*resh strawberries create a divine granita.

1 cup water

1/2 cup sugar

2-1/2 cups fresh, ripe strawberries

In a large saucepan, bring water and sugar to a boil over medium heat, stirring until sugar dissolves. As soon as mixture starts to boil, reduce heat to medium and allow mixture to cook exactly 5 minutes. Remove from heat and cool to room temperature.

Place strawberries in a food processor; pulse briefly until they become pulp.

As soon as sugar-water mixture is completely cooled, stir in strawberry pulp; pour into a 9 x 5-inch loaf pan. Place in freezer for 3 hours, stirring every half hour to allow the ice that forms around the sides and bottom of pan to blend into the part that is still liquid. When mixture freezes into a firm, snowy slush, remove from freezer and serve.

Makes about 1-1/2 pints of granita.

Spumoni

Spumoni

I created this *spumoni* in memory of the kind I used to buy from a stand on Chicago's Near West Side.

- 1 (16 oz.) jar of maraschino cherries, drained
- 3 cups whipping cream, room temperature
- 2 tablespoons Amaretto liqueur
- 2 tablespoons orange zest
- 7 egg yolks
- 3/4 cup sugar
- 1 cup semisweet chocolate chips
- 3/4 cup coarsely chopped pistachios
- 1/4 cup chopped candied citron

Slice drained maraschino cherries and set aside. In a large saucepan, bring the whipping cream, Amaretto and orange zest to a boil over low heat; then remove from heat and set aside.

In a large mixer bowl, beat egg yolks and sugar 3 minutes; then stir cream-Amaretto mixture into the egg yolks until well blended. Return mixture to the saucepan and cook over very low heat, stirring constantly with a wooden spoon until mixture is thick enough to coat the spoon lightly, about 5 minutes. Do not let the mixture boil or it will curdle and turn lumpy.

Remove mixture from heat and set aside; cool to room temperature. Stir maraschino cherries, chocolate chips, pistachios and citron into the cream mixture. Then pack a 2-quart ice-cream freezer with layers of cracked ice and coarse rock salt as recommended by the freezer manufacturer. Pour the completely cooled gelato mixture into the ice-cream can. Cover.

Turn electric ice-cream maker on and churn about 50 minutes or until motor slows or stops. If using a hand ice-cream maker, let stand for 3 to 4 minutes before turning handle. Do not stop churning until gelato becomes solid or mixture will turn lumpy.

To harden or ripen the gelato, scrape mixture from sides of can toward the bottom, place a piece of plastic wrap on the surface, and cover tightly. Place in freezer 2 hours.

Makes about 2 pints.

Lemon Ice

Granita di Limone

My grandmother's recipe for *granita di limone* was similar to any you would find today in Sicily. Her trademark was the grated lemon zest she added for even more lemon flavor. It is essential to use freshly squeezed lemon juice.

> **2 cups water**
>
> **1 cup sugar**
>
> **1 cup lemon juice (4-5 fresh lemons)**
>
> **1 tablespoon lemon zest**

In a large saucepan, bring water and sugar to a boil over medium heat, stirring until sugar dissolves. As soon as mixture starts to boil, reduce heat to medium and allow mixture to cook exactly 5 minutes. Remove from heat and cool to room temperature.

As soon as mixture is completely cooled, stir in lemon juice and lemon zest; then pour into a 9 x 5-inch loaf pan. Place in freezer for 3 hours, stirring every half hour to allow the ice that forms around the sides and bottom of pan to blend into the part that is still liquid. When mixture freezes into firm, snowy slush, remove from freezer and serve.

Makes about 1-1/2 pints of granita.

Mango Peach Ice

Granita di Mango

*U*se only very ripe fresh mangoes and peaches for full-bodied flavor. The flecks of peach skin also add color.

1-1/2 cups water

1/2 cup granulated sugar

1/4 cup brown sugar

2 mangoes, peeled and chopped

2 peaches, sliced, unpeeled and chopped

In a large saucepan, bring water and sugar to a boil over medium heat, stirring until sugar dissolves. As soon as mixture starts to boil, reduce heat to medium and allow mixture to cook exactly 5 minutes. Remove pan from heat and allow to cool to room temperature.

Place mangoes and peaches in a food processor, pulse briefly to crush into pulp.

As soon as sugar-water mixture is completely cooled, stir in mango-peach pulp; then pour into a 9 x 5-inch loaf pan. Place in freezer for 3 hours, stirring every half hour to allow the ice that forms around the sides and bottom of pan to blend into the part that is still liquid. When mixture freezes into a firm, snowy slush, remove from freezer and serve.

Makes about 2-1/2 pints.

Mocha Latte Ice

Granita di Mocha-Latte

*H*ere is another way to enjoy the rich flavors of espresso and cocoa, especially during warm weather.

> 3 cups espresso or strong coffee
>
> 1/3 cup sugar
>
> 1 cup whipping cream
>
> 1 tablespoon unsweetened cocoa

In a large saucepan, bring espresso, sugar, whipping cream and unsweetened cocoa to a boil over medium heat, stirring until sugar dissolves. As soon as mixture starts to boil, reduce heat to medium and allow mixture to cook exactly 5 minutes. Remove pan from heat and cool to room temperature.

As soon as mixture is completely cooled, pour it into a 9 x 5-inch loaf pan. Place in freezer for 3 hours, stirring every half hour to allow the ice that forms around the sides and bottom of pan to blend into the part that is still liquid. When mixture freezes into a firm slush, remove from freezer and serve.

Makes about 2 pints.

Raspberry Lemon Granita
Granita di Lamponi e limone

*L*emon zest and fresh raspberry pulp are well-matched flavors in this granita.

> 1 cup water
>
> 1/2 cup sugar
>
> 3 cups fresh raspberries
>
> 1 tablespoon lemon zest

In a large saucepan, bring water and sugar to a boil over medium heat, stirring until sugar dissolves. As soon as mixture starts to boil, reduce heat to medium and allow mixture to cook exactly 5 minutes. Remove pan from heat and allow to cool to room temperature.

Place raspberries in a food processor, pulse briefly to crush berries.

As soon as sugar-water mixture is completely cooled, stir in raspberry pulp and lemon zest; then pour into a 9 x 5-inch loaf pan. Place in freezer for 3 hours, stirring every half hour to allow the ice that forms around the sides and bottom of pan to blend into the part that is still liquid. When mixture freezes into a firm, snowy slush, remove from freezer and serve.

Makes about 2 pints.

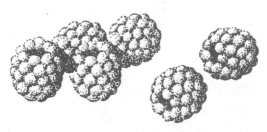

Cream and Custard Desserts

Dolci di Crema e Budino

*E*ating one's way through Italy's glorious cream and custard desserts is like touring different regions of Italy. Each cream or custard can best be described as *eclectic*—reflecting the individual character of each region.

Drawing from the best, I start with a contribution from Piedmont's Valle d'Aosta. The name *Fiandolein* indicates the heavy Austrian cultural influence over the area. Fiandolein is made with whipping cream, egg yolks, sugar, rum and lemon peel poured into a bowl of leftover bread, fruit and nuts.

Southeast of Valle d'Aosta is Milan, home of some of Italy's most delicate creams, such as Chilled Vanilla Cream or *Bonett de Lattemiele*—perfect when served with summer's fresh fruit.

Northwest of Venice lies Treviso, a city known for its canals, frescos and a creamed, layered dessert so popular it has been appropriated by North American culture. *Tiramisu,* a literal translation of "pick-me-up," is concocted out of layers of sponge cake soaked in brewed espresso-chocolate and filled with either mascarpone or cream cheese.

Perhaps the quintessential dessert of Italy is Sicily's *Zabaglione,* which is in a category of being both cream and custard, flavored with wine. Though Zagablione is great by itself, it also lends glory to many pastries and cakes.

Cream-Bread Pudding

Fiandolein

*I*n the Valle d'Aosta, a cream made of milk, egg yolks, sugar, rum and lemon peel called *Fiandolein* is poured over leftover bread. As in bread pudding, my version is poured over leftover Italian or French bread, diced mission figs and dates, raisins and walnuts. Fiandolein is great when served warm or cold with a jug of milk or whipping cream.

    1/2 lb. Italian bread, torn into 1-inch pieces

    1/4 cup dried mission figs, diced

    1/4 cup dates, diced

    1/4 cup black raisins

    1/4 cup coarsely chopped walnuts

    1/4 cup butter

    1-1/2 cups milk

    1-1/2 cups whipping cream

    1/2 cup granulated sugar

    3 whole eggs

    1-1/2 teaspoons dark rum

    1/4 teaspoon ground nutmeg

    1 tablespoon lemon zest

    2 tablespoons granulated sugar

    Milk or whipping cream

Preheat oven to 350F (180C). You will need an ungreased 13 x 9 x 2-inch baking dish, preferably glass. Place bread pieces in dish; then sprinkle figs, dates, raisins and walnuts evenly over bread pieces. In a medium-size saucepan, heat butter, milk and whipping cream until butter is melted. Stir; remove from heat and set aside.

In a medium bowl, with an electric mixer, beat 1/4 cup granulated sugar, eggs, dark rum, nutmeg and lemon zest until smooth. Add milk and cream mixture, stir until thoroughly blended.

Pour over bread and fruit; then sprinkle 2 tablespoons granulated sugar over mixture. Place dish inside a larger pan, add about 1 inch of very hot water. Place in oven. Bake 40-45 minutes or until wooden pick inserted into pudding comes out clean. Set aside to cool 30 minutes. Serve warm with a jug of milk or whipping cream. May also be served cold.

Makes 12 servings.

Pick-Me-Up

Tiramisu

❧⚜❧

*Y*ou may opt for either Italian *mascarpone,* available in some markets, or a good-quality cream cheese. Two variations of tiramisu are provided, depending on the cheese.

Mascarpone is richer, with close to 80 percent milkfat, while most cream-cheese brands contain around 45 percent. Mascarpone obviously yields a richer-tasting product, but I find that using a good-quality cream cheese produces an equally good tiramisu.

Note: Average cost of mascarpone, $8 to $10 per pound, is much higher than the price of cream cheese.

Cake:

6 whole eggs, separated

2/3 cup powdered sugar

1 teaspoon vanilla

2/3 cup cake flour

Filling: (2 choices)

1. *Cream-cheese filling:*

1-3/4 cups whipping cream

2-1/4 cups cream cheese or 2-1/2 (8-oz.) packages, room temperature

1-3/4 cup powdered sugar

2-1/2 tablespoons Marsala

1/2 teaspoon vanilla extract

2. *Mascarpone filling:*

1-3/4 cups whipping cream

1-3/4 cups powdered sugar

2-1/2 tablespoons Marsala

1/2 teaspoon vanilla extract

2 cups (1 lb.) Mascarpone cheese

Brewed Espresso or Coffee Soak:

1 cup brewed espresso or strong coffee, room temperature

2 teaspoons granulated sugar

Garnish:

1 (8-oz.) bar bittersweet chocolate

9 whole strawberries

To Prepare Cake: Preheat oven to 375F (190C). Coat a 13 x 9-inch baking pan with vegetable-oil spray and flour. Beat egg yolks with an electric mixer until thick and foamy; then set aside. In a large bowl, whip egg whites and 2/3 cup powdered sugar with an electric mixer until stiff peaks form; gradually fold in egg yolks and vanilla with a rubber spatula. Fold in cake flour with a rubber spatula until well blended. Pour and spread batter evenly in prepared baking pan.

Bake 12 minutes or until wooden pick inserted into center comes out clean. Remove from oven and let cool 5 minutes. Then gently loosen cake with a metal spatula and invert onto rack to cool completely before adding filling.

To Prepare Cream-Cheese Filling (Variation 1):   In a medium-size bowl, using an electric mixer beat whipping cream until soft peaks form, then set aside.

In a large bowl, with an electric mixer beat the cream cheese and 1-3/4 cup powdered sugar until smooth and just beginning to get stiff. **Do not overbeat or the cheese will curdle!** At medium speed, add whipped cream; then add Marsala and vanilla until stiff peaks hold. Set aside; refrigerate until chilled.   *(Recipe continued on page 124)*

To Prepare Mascarpone Filling (Variation 2):   In a large bowl, with an electric mixer, beat whipping cream, 1-3/4 cups powdered sugar, Marsala and vanilla until soft peaks form.

In a food processor, using a steel blade soften the mascarpone with several pulses until smooth; then add to whipped-cream mixture while continuing to beat until stiff. Set aside; refrigerate until chilled.

To Assemble Tiramisu: You will need an ungreased 8- or 9-inch baking dish (preferably glass) to make a good presentation of tiramisu.

With a serrated knife, cut cooled sponge cake into two equal layers, then place one layer on bottom of dish. Using a spoon, pour half of the brewed espresso or coffee sweetened with sugar over surface of cake layer. Next, spoon and spread evenly half of chilled cream-and-cheese filling. Top with second layer of cake; repeat with remaining espresso or coffee and cream-and-cheese filling. After smoothing top layer, shave bittersweet chocolate bar across the tiramisu. For a perfect garnish, top each portion with a fresh, whole strawberry. Serve immediately or refrigerate until ready to serve. Can be stored in refrigerator, covered with plastic wrap, for up to two days.

Makes about 9 servings.

Vanilla Cream
Bonett de Lattemiele

This creamy, chilled Milanese classic starts with vanilla and lemon zest and is the perfect foil to fresh fruit.

> **2 (1/4-oz.) envelopes unflavored gelatin**
> **1/3 cup cold water**

Milk-Egg Mixture:
> **2-1/4 cups milk**
> **3/4 cup granulated sugar**
> **6 egg yolks**
> **1 teaspoon cornstarch**
> **1 teaspoon vanilla extract**
> **2 teaspoons lemon zest**
> **2 cups whipping cream**

Garnish:
> **Sliced strawberries, peaches, nectarines, plums or raspberries.**

Lightly coat an 8-cup ring mold or Bundt pan with vegetable-oil spray. In a small bowl, soak gelatin in cold water about 5 minutes; place gelatin and water over low heat to dissolve completely. Remove from heat and set aside.

In a large bowl, using an electric mixer, blend milk, granulated sugar, egg yolks, cornstarch, vanilla, and lemon zest until frothy. Place milk-egg mixture in a medium-size saucepan over medium heat and stir constantly until temperature reaches about 170F (75C) on a candy thermometer. It must be thickened enough to coat the back of a spoon.

Remove saucepan from heat; then stir in dissolved gelatin. Set aside to cool about 5 minutes; then transfer saucepan to refrigerator for 15 minutes, or until mixture is cooled to room temperature.

Meanwhile, in a large bowl, using an electric mixer, beat whipping cream until soft peaks form. Remove milk-egg mixture from refrigerator. Fold whipped cream into cooled milk-egg mixture with a rubber spatula until thoroughly blended. Pour into mold. Refrigerate at least 6 hours, unmold and garnish with fruit before serving.

Makes 10-12 servings.

Variations

Chocolate Vanilla Cream

Crema al cioccolato

Reduce milk to 2 cups and add 2 squares of unsweetened chocolate.

Raspberry-Orange Cream with orange liqueur

Crema di Lamponi e liquore di arancia

Reduce milk to 2 cups and omit vanilla and lemon zest. Add 1/4 cup raspberry preserves and 2 tablespoons Cointreau liqueur.

Custard with Marsala

Zabaglione

*O*ne of the most sublime and renowned of Italian custards or creams is Zabaglione, also spelled Zabaione, originating in Sicily. This very basic recipe features Marsala, egg yolks, sugar and whipping cream.

3 egg yolks

1/2 cup powdered sugar

1/4 cup Marsala

1-1/4 cups whipping cream

In a medium-size bowl, using an electric mixer, beat egg yolks and powdered sugar until creamy. Beat in Marsala, 1 tablespoon at a time, until thoroughly blended.

Place egg-yolk-and-Marsala mixture in a double boiler over low heat and whisk until thick and creamy. Remove from heat and set aside to cool completely.

Meanwhile, in a medium-size bowl, using an electric mixer whip whipping cream until stiff peaks form. When egg-yolk-and-Marsala mixture is cooled completely, fold in whipped cream with a rubber spatula. Blend thoroughly, pour into individual serving cups and refrigerate until serving.

Makes about 4 cups.

Puffed Pastry with Zabaglione
Pasta Sfogliata con Zabaglione

*H*aving a summer party and need a simple, crowd-size dessert? Try spooning zabaglione cream onto individual portions of frozen puffed pastry; and top with a fine layer of finely ground hazelnuts. Garnish with fresh strawberries.

1 recipe Zabaglione (page 127)

1-1/3 sheets of frozen puff pastry from a (17-1/4- oz.) package, completely thawed.

1/3 cup coarse hazelnut crumbs

Garnish:

16 large fresh strawberries

Prepare Zabaglione according to instructions and refrigerate in a large bowl instead of in individual cups. Preheat oven to 350F (180C). You will need a large, ungreased cookie sheet. Unfold completely thawed puff pastry on a lightly floured surface. Divide pastry in half; then roll each half into two long rectangles, each measuring about 6-1/2 x 10-1/2 inches.

On first rectangle of pastry, cut in half lengthwise; then cut each half into 4 equal portions. Repeat for the second rectangle. Place 16 puff-pastry portions on an ungreased cookie sheet about 1/2 inch apart.

Bake for 15 minutes or until golden brown. Remove puff pastry from oven and carefully transfer to rack to cool completely.

Just before serving, spoon onto each pastry a generous portion of chilled Zabaglione Top each serving with a generous sprinkling of hazelnuts and a fresh, whole strawberry.

Makes 16 individual servings.

Tuscan Meringue with Strawberries

Meringa alla Toscana con le Fragole

Here an Italian meringue shell encases fresh strawberries and tops them with dollops of a yogurt cream with a hint of orange liqueur. I'm calling this a *Tuscan Meringue* because in Italy, strawberries are grown prolifically in the Garfagnana district of Tuscany.

Orange Yogurt Cream:

1-1/3 cups vanilla yogurt, thoroughly drained

1 (8-oz.) package cream cheese

5 tablespoons powdered sugar

1 tablespoon Cointreau liqueur

Meringue Shell:

5 egg whites

1/4 teaspoon cream of tartar

1 cup granulated sugar

1/4 teaspoon cinnamon

Strawberry Filling:

4 cups of fresh, sliced strawberries

2 tablespoons honey

To Prepare Orange-Yogurt Cream: In a large bowl, using an electric mixer, whip yogurt, cream cheese, powdered sugar and Cointreau at low speed about 10 minutes. Set aside and refrigerate.

To Prepare Meringue Shell: Preheat oven to 275F (140C). Line a large baking sheet with parchment paper. In a large bowl, with an electric mixer, beat egg whites and cream of tartar until foamy. Beat in granulated sugar, 1 tablespoon at a time, and cinnamon on high speed until meringue is stiff and very glossy.

On parchment-lined baking sheet, spread and shape meringue into a 9-inch-square shell. Using a rubber spatula, build and shape a 3/4-inch rim along sides of shell to enclose the fresh strawberries. Bake 1-1/2 hours. Turn off oven; leave meringue shell in closed oven for 1 hour longer; then transfer to baking sheet to cool completely.

To Assemble Tuscan Meringue: In a large bowl, using a wooden spoon, gently mix sliced strawberries and honey. Spoon and spread evenly inside cooled meringue shell. Slice in rectangular servings and top with dollops of chilled orange-yogurt cream.

Makes 8-10 servings.

Fried Pastries and Cream Puffs

Dolci Fritti e Bignè

*W*hen spoonfuls of cream-puff paste, or *pasta bignè,* are puffed in hot oil and rolled in sugar, they become *sfinci.* And when sfinci are rolled in cinnamon-sugar and walnut or pecans, they become *Sfinci alla Calabrese,* rivaling their French counterpart, *beignet* from New Orleans.

But when spoonfuls of pasta bignè are baked, then stuffed with a creamy ricotta-fruit filling, they become St. Joseph's Day Cream Puffs or *Bignè di San Giuseppe,* thereby reaching divine status.

Divine best describes Italian fried pastries, fritters and cream puffs. Cannoli, for example, are horn-rimmed, deep-fried pastries (*dolci fritti*) stuffed with a sweet-ricotta filling made with chocolate chips and an orange liqueur. Its richness reflects the kind of luxury one saves for rare and special occasions.

Celebrations are the perfect times for serving any of these rich delicacies. And when the event calls for a brunch, the Neopolitan Brandy Fritters, or *Sfinci Alla Napoletana,* are an intriguing alternative to pancakes or waffles.

Pasta Bignè Batter

Pasta bignè, the cream-puff paste featured in some recipes for fritters or cream puffs, is very simple to work with, particularly when using an electric mixer to achieve a smooth, pasty texture.

Cannoli

Cannoli

*C*annoli were once referred to by Sicilians as Turkish heads, or *testa di turco*. The shells of the cannoli are stuffed with sweet ricotta filling flecked with coarsely chopped pistachios and toasted coconut. You will need cannoli tubes to fry the shells.

Filling:

1 (15-oz.) container ricotta cheese
1 (3-oz.) package cream cheese, room temperature
1 teaspoon vanilla extract
1 tablespoon Cointreau liqueur
1 cup powdered sugar
3/4 cup semisweet chocolate chips

Pastry Shell:

2-1/2 cups all-purpose flour
1 tablespoon granulated sugar
1-1/2 tablespoons unsweetened cocoa powder
1/4 cup cold butter, cut into small pieces
2 teaspoons brewed espresso or strong coffee
1 egg yolk
1/2 cup plus 2 tablespoons Port wine
1-1/3 cups canola oil for deep frying

Garnish:

1/4 cup coarsely chopped pistachios
1/2 cup shredded coconut
or
9 maraschino cherries
Powdered sugar

To Prepare Cannoli Filling: In a large bowl, with an electric mixer beat ricotta cheese, cream cheese, vanilla, Cointreau and powdered sugar until smooth. Turn off mixer and gently stir in semisweet chocolate chips. Refrigerate to chill until ready to assemble cannoli.

To Prepare Cannoli Pastry Shell: In another large bowl, combine flour, granulated sugar and cocoa. Using a pastry blender or two knives, cut butter into dry ingredients until evenly distributed and mixture becomes crumbly (or use the paddle attachment of an electric mixer set at low speed). Make a well in the center and pour in espresso or coffee, egg yolk and Port wine. Continue mixing until dough clings together. Gather dough into a mound and wrap in foil or plastic wrap. Refrigerate and chill at least 30 minutes.

Remove dough from refrigerator. On a lightly floured surface, roll out dough to a 12-inch-square rectangle, slightly over 1/8 inch thick. Cut dough into nine 4-inch squares. Using a rolling pin, round off 2 opposite corners of each square.

Twist each pastry square around a lightly greased cannoli tube, joining the non-rounded corners; press dough with fingertips and thumbs to seal securely.

In a large, deep skillet, heat oil to 375F (190C). Fry each pastry-covered tube about 3 minutes or until golden brown, using tongs to turn frequently. Remove from oil; drain well on paper towels. Cool slightly; then remove metal tubes. Place pastry shells on rack to cool completely.

To Assemble Cannoli: Sprinkle shredded coconut in an ungreased heavy skillet over medium-low heat. Stir constantly until golden brown—about 5 minutes. Remove from heat and set aside.

Remove ricotta filling from refrigerator. Using a tiny spoon or piping bag, fill cooled cannoli shells Decorate open ends with pistachios and toasted coconut. Or top each cannoli with a maraschino cherry and a light sprinkle of powdered sugar.

Makes 9 cannoli shells.

Calabrian Wine Fritters

Sfinci alla Calabrese

*I*n Calabria, these wine fritters are usually coated in honey. I've opted for a coating combining finely chopped walnuts or pecans, sugar and cinnamon.

Topping:

3/4 cup granulated sugar

1/2 teaspoon ground cinnamon

1/3 cup finely chopped walnuts or pecans

Cream Puff Paste or Pasta Bignè:

1/2 cup Marsala

1/2 cup water

8 tablespoons butter

1/3 cup granulated sugar

1 cup all-purpose flour

3 whole eggs

1-1/4 cup canola oil for frying

In a medium-size bowl, sift together 3/4 cup granulated sugar and cinnamon. Add finely chopped walnuts or pecans; stir with two forks until mixture is well blended. Set aside.

In a large saucepan, bring the Marsala, water, butter and 1/3 cup sugar to a boil. Remove from heat and add flour. Stir until smooth; then return the pan to heat briefly (a few seconds) until the mixture turns into a pasty consistency and doesn't stick to sides of pan. Immediately remove from heat. Using an electric mixer, beat in whole eggs one at a time at medium speed until mixture is smooth and pasty.

In a large, deep skillet, heat oil to 375F (190C). Drop in mixture by tablespoonfuls several at a time and fry until puffy and golden brown (about 3 minutes). Remove with slotted spoon. Drain on paper towels; then immediately roll hot fritters in bowl of sugar-cinnamon-nut mixture until well coated. Serve warm.

Makes about 36 fritters.

St. Joseph's Cream Puffs
Bignè di San Giuseppe

On March 19, many Italians and Italian Americans celebrate with a cream puff filled with ricotta and orange zest. My version contains a hint of chocolate-mint in the filling.

Filling:

1 lb. ricotta cheese

3-1/2 tablespoons powdered sugar

2 tablespoons milk

1 tablespoon orange zest

1/3 cup chopped candied citron, candied orange,
    or a combination of both

2 tablespoons grated chocolate-mint bar

Cream-Puff Paste or Pasta Bignè:

1 cup water

1/2 cup butter

1 cup flour

1/4 cup powdered sugar

4 whole eggs

Topping:

2 tablespoons powdered sugar

In a large bowl, using an electric mixer, beat ricotta cheese, 3-1/2 table-spoons powdered sugar, milk and orange zest together until creamy. Add citron or orange and grated chocolate mint; continue beating until mixture is smooth and creamy. Refrigerate until ready to assemble cream puffs.

Preheat oven to 400F (200C). Lightly coat a large baking sheet with vegetable-oil spray. In a large saucepan, bring water and butter to a boil. Remove from heat and add flour and 1/4 cup sugar. Stir until smooth; then return the pan to heat briefly (a few seconds) until the mixture turns into a pasty consistency and doesn't stick to the sides of the pan. Immediately remove from heat. Using an electric mixer, beat in eggs one at a time at medium speed until mixture is smooth and pasty.

Drop heaping tablespoonfuls of mixture onto baking sheet, 2-1/2 to 3 inches apart. Bake for 10 minutes. Then reduce temperature to 350F (180C) and bake about 15 minutes longer or until puffs turn golden brown. Remove from oven and cool on rack.

When completely cooled, using a sharp knife, cut off the tops of puffs. Remove ricotta filling from refrigerator and fill the inside of puffs. Then replace tops of puffs and sprinkle with powdered sugar.

Makes 24 small cream puffs.

Neopolitan Brandy Fritters
Sfinci Alla Napoletana

Neopolitan-style brandy fritters are made from a hazelnut batter enriched with ricotta cheese and raisins. Serve with sprinkles of fresh lemon juice and powdered sugar for the most heavenly fritter you will ever eat.

> **2 cups self-rising flour**
>
> **1/2 cup finely chopped hazelnuts**
>
> **1/2 cup sugar**
>
> **1/4 teaspoon salt**
>
> **1 lb. ricotta cheese**
>
> **6 whole eggs, well beaten**
>
> **1-1/2 tablespoons brandy**
>
> **1/2 cup raisins**
>
> **1-1/4 cups canola oil for frying**

> Topping:
>
> **2 lemons, cut into halves, for squeezing on fritters**
>
> **3-1/2 to 4 tablespoons sifted powdered sugar**

In a large bowl, combine self-rising flour, chopped hazelnuts, sugar and salt. Make a well in the center and spoon in ricotta cheese; then pour in beaten eggs and brandy. Add raisins. Using an electric mixer, mix all ingredients for two minutes or until batter is smooth and creamy.

In a large, deep skillet, heat oil to 375F (190C). Drop in batter by tablespoonfuls several at a time and fry until puffy and golden (about 3 minutes). Remove with slotted spoon. Drain on paper towels; repeat with remaining batter. Sprinkle lemon juice and sifted powdered sugar on top of hot fritters and serve.

Makes about 66 fritters.

Index
English and Italian

English Index

Italian Index